PARENT TALK

50

Quick,

Effective

Solutions to

the Most Common

Parenting Challenges

**Stanley Shapiro
and Karen Skinulis**

with Richard Skinulis
Illustrated by Graham Pilsworth

Stoddart

TORONTO • BUFFALO

Published in 1997 by
Stoddart Publishing Co. Limited

Distributed in Canada by
General Distribution Services Inc.
30 Lesmill Road
Toronto, Canada M3B 2T6
Tel. (416) 445-3333
Fax (416) 445-5967
e-mail Customer.Service@ccmailgw.genpub.com

Distributed in the United States by
General Distribution Services Inc.
85 River Rock Drive, Suite 202
Buffalo, New York 14207
Toll-free Tel. 1-800-805-1083
Toll-free Fax 1-800-481-6207
e-mail gdsinc@genpub.com

01   00   99   98   97   1   2   3   4   5

Cataloging in Publication Data

Shapiro, Stanley, 1934–
Parent talk: 50 quick, effective solutions to the most common parenting challenges

ISBN 0-7737-5858-5

1. Child rearing. I. Skinulis, Karen, 1960–
II. Skinulis, Richard, 1947–   III. Title.

HQ769.S53   1997   649'.1   97-930319-2

Illustrations: Graham Pilsworth
Cover design: Pekoe Jones/*multiphrenia*
Text Design: Tannice Goddard
Printed and bound in Canada

CONTENTS

CONTENTS

A Message for Frazzled Parents

We're going to cut to the chase. You're reading this book because you have a problem with your kid, and you want to know how to fix it. In *Parent Talk*, we address fifty of the most common parenting problems, so you should be able to find a chapter that offers clear, concise, and practical advice specific to your current dilemma. But you should know that almost any child-rearing problem — not just those contained in this book — can be solved if you pay attention to, and act upon, the following basic precepts:

1. Understand the motivation of your children's misbehaviour. What goal or payoff are they seeking?
2. Let children experience the consequences of their choices.
3. Treat children with respect, no matter how disrespectful their own behaviour may be.
4. Encourage your children. Do what you can to bolster their self-esteem.

We briefly expand on these core ideas below. To get the most out of this book, we recommend that you read on before turning to the individual solutions. We also recommend that you make these basic principles an integral part of your approach to parenting.

The Goals — Why Kids Are Uncooperative

Any parent who has watched their child whack his sister over the head with a broom for the tenth time, even though he knows he will get in trouble for it, has asked the same question: "Why is he *doing* that?"

Actually, the answer is fairly simple — to achieve one of four goals: UNDUE ATTENTION, POWER, REVENGE, or ASSUMED INADEQUACY. If they attain their goal — by not eating or by throwing apples at your neighbour or by turning bedtime into a hell on earth — then they will do it again and again no matter what you do in retaliation. They are uncooperative, in other words, not *despite* what you do but *because* of it.

Undue Attention

This kid only feels significant when she is the centre of attention, even if that attention consists of someone angrily threatening to ground her for the rest of her life. This can result from neglect or (more often) when a child is shown too much attention at a very young age. After a while they can't live without it, and uncooperative or inappropriate behaviour is one of the most sure-fire ways to get it. If your kid is annoying you, if you keep thinking things like "I wish she'd buzz off," and if the behaviour stops when you yell at her, her goal is probably attention. The solution is to give her attention when her behaviour is socially acceptable, and ignore her when it's not. Eventually you can wean her off the undue attention altogether.

Power

Winning is what this kid is after — *what* he wins is not so important. He feels significant when he can either ignore a command or get you to give in to one of his. If you feel angry and frustrated when dealing with him, if he still does it after you have corrected him, and if you are walking around thinking "I'll show *him* who's boss," your kid is into power. You need to turn his desire to lead and be in control into a desire to help the family. Don't fight with him. Ask for his opinion. Make taking out the garbage *his* decision.

Revenge

The revengeful kid feels her parents don't like her, and she wants to hurt them. This can follow hard on the heels of a power struggle where punishment has been used by the parents in order to win the war. If you feel hurt, if you have negative feelings about her, and if you wonder to yourself "How could she *do* that to me?" it's revenge. The cure is to give her lots of love and affection instead of punishment and a tongue-lashing. Work on repairing the damaged relationship.

Assumed Inadequacy

This kid believes that he is not very good at things, so he sees no use in trying. He is discouraged but paradoxically could also be extremely ambitious (a deadly combination). To avoid trying anything new, he must convince everyone else that he is incompetent. His goal can be summed up in the oft-heard phrase: "Leave me alone!"

If you find that you have given up teaching him anything or expecting anything from him, you can bet his goal is inadequacy. The solution is to give him a lot of encouragement in order to improve his self-esteem.

In general, the best strategy for all uncooperative or inappropriate behaviour is to stop giving your kids a payoff. You have to learn to withhold your anger and stay loving even when they are pushing your buttons. Make sure you keep your tone friendly when you talk to them about it. This is easy to say and hard to do after a typical day in the rat race for most of us. But the reality is that they are usually doing it unconsciously, and knowing this should help you keep your cool. Also, most parents talk too much when there is a problem, as if they could use logic to prove they are right. Talk less and act more.

Your Strategy — Using Consequences

The fact that there is a consequence for nearly every human action is the best thing that ever happened to parents. When it comes to kids, there are two kinds of consequences: Natural and Logical.

Natural Consequences

As the name suggests, these are things that happen naturally when your kids do or don't do something — without any interference on your part.

For example:

- If you leave your baseball glove out in the rain, it will get ruined.
- If you don't eat your dinner, you are hungry.
- If you don't wear your coat to school, you freeze your little buns off.

Logical Consequences

Sometimes natural consequences are too dangerous or inappropriate, so you have to come up with consequences that have a logical connection to the behaviour you are trying to correct. The parents engineer these consequences to teach children that their actions have repercussions, and that they are responsible for their own behaviour.

For example:

- If you won't stop playing in the street, you have to stay in the house.
- If you won't get ready to go to Grandma's, you can't come at all.
- If you freak out at the mall in front of hundreds of shoppers, you have to go home and you can't go to the mall again until you can act appropriately.

For natural and logical consequences to work, the following rules must be followed:

1. The consequence must be related to the behaviour.
2. Choices must be given whenever possible.
3. The child must know there will be a second chance to improve.
4. Your attitude must be instructive and your tone friendly. This will be easier if you don't let your ego or your emotions get involved in the problem. If you feel yourself getting angry, it's not a good time to try to arrange logical consequences.

Respect — Not Punishment

Punishment is subtly, but very importantly, different from consequences. Where consequences have a direct correlation to a child's actions, punishment is arbitrary: "You can't watch TV because you didn't eat your dinner." "Oh, I see," the kid thinks, "you just want to make me suffer." So punishment, while momentarily satisfying for parents (especially when they are angry), doesn't actually *teach* kids anything. They know that they shouldn't do something, but they don't know *why* they shouldn't do it.

The worst thing about punishment, however, is that it is both discouraging and disrespectful. Punishment tells your kids they have messed up and let you down, and this is discouraging to them. The disrespect comes from the parents exerting their will over the child, often in a humiliating way. Even what some people refer to as "a little slap on the behind" is disrespectful. We believe that you should treat children with the same respect that you would like to be treated with yourself. For these reasons, we don't believe in corporal punishment.

Another danger of punishment is that it can make your child dislike you. It can become a battle between two people — my will against yours — while the effective use of consequences places the emphasis on the child and the current situation.

Encouragement — Towards Higher Self-Esteem

We saved the most important part of parenting for last. Encouragement makes children feel good about themselves (even when they have made a mistake) and discouragement makes them feel that no matter what they do, they will never be good enough.

One way to deal with misbehaviour and failure is to separate what the person has done from the person who has done it. For example, if your child drops a glass of milk, don't tell them how careless they are. Instead, try a more positive approach: "I see you had a problem with the milk. Let's clean it up and try again." This turns a potentially discouraging accident into a learning experience.

We can be encouraging in everything we do. In fact, the difference between an encouraging and discouraging statement or action can be quite subtle. It could be, for example, the difference between saying "That's not bad, but if you did this and that, it would be perfect" (discouraging) and "That looks great, you really seemed to be getting a kick out of doing it" (encouraging).

A Note About Family Democracy

The Authoritarian Age is dead. Today we live in the Age of Democracy, which Winston Churchill called "the worst system — except for all the rest." It is taking some of us a little time to grasp the fact that people in our society are moving towards social equality. This is particularly hard when it comes to our kids. "Kids aren't my equal," you huff indignantly. "I'm bigger and smarter and have way more money than them." All of which is true. But equality doesn't mean that everyone is the *same*. We all have different levels of knowledge, experience, physical strength, and skills. When we embrace the notion of equality, we have respect for all people, and treat them with the dignity they are entitled to as members of the human race.

The key to the democratic process, in any context, including parenting, is the sharing of decision-making. This is the hard part. Ask any dictator — absolute power is hard to give up. But how will your kids know how to solve problems or learn from their mistakes if you do it all for them?

Making decisions together, and following through on them, brings families closer together. It also alleviates the constant bickering that can turn the lives of some families into third rate sitcoms — without the laugh track. But this decision-making process needs a structure. That structure is the family meeting.

The Family Meeting

Anyone who has held one of their kids' birthday parties at home knows how close children can come to total, chaotic anarchy. Kids need a structure. It's good for them. It teaches them about order and lets them know their limits. The family meeting provides the structure that kids need, as well as a forum for their ideas and concerns. It's also a fair and non-confrontational way of solving family disputes, infinitely better than the familiar parent–child tugs of war or sibling rivalries that mar the life of many families.

These meetings should be held regularly — say every Saturday after lunch or some other convenient time. Here are some tips:

- Keep adding to the agenda all week so everything gets covered.
- Rotate the Chair so the kids don't feel like you've stacked the deck against them.
- Start off with "what's going right" so it doesn't end up as a gripe session.
- Talk things out until everyone agrees to new rules, menus, or plans, even if they only agree to try it.
- Make sure everyone knows that the rule can be changed at the next meeting.

Getting the kids to agree takes a lot of the pressure off you, but it's not easy. Don't dominate the meetings with the "right" (read "your") suggestions or the kids will never buy into this process. Instead, make observations about problems around the house, and ask open-ended questions about how they could be solved. Work towards a consensus, not a majority. Once they get into it, you'll be surprised how seriously your kids take these meetings.

An Encouraging Word

The most important thing to remember is that parents should always work at making things *better*, rather than *perfect*. To accomplish this you need a plan. Used with consistency, the concise strategies you learn in this book will allow you to deal with problems the moment they arise, and to encourage your children to be part of the solution. This might not turn your kids into perfect little angels, but it will put your family on the road to a much better future.

BEHAVIOUR
UNBECOMING...

1

DAWDLING
The Slow Motion Kid

The Behaviour It's always amazing to watch a child who normally zooms around at top speed suddenly turn into a three-toed sloth when *you're* in a hurry. The parent rushes around like a lunatic getting everyone dressed, with one eye glued to a clock that is ticking closer and closer to the stroke of doom. The kids, on the other hand, suddenly become fascinated with the weave of the carpet, or something they recently excavated from their nose. And it doesn't just happen when it's time to get ready for school — they can also turn a twenty-minute walk into a two-hour exploration of every caterpillar and puddle they see.

Why They Do It Sometimes it's deliberate — a way for toddlers to assert their independence — while at other times

it's quite innocent. In fact, most dawdling is not misbehaviour at all, but rather the result of the fact that kids have a different sense of time than adults. Kids live in the present, with little understanding of the future. Dawdling only gets nasty when they are doing it either for attention or because they feel you are badgering them to go faster.

Your Reaction

The usual result of all this dawdling is that you are forced to either play the grouchy prison guard, or live your life according to the rhythms of a three-year-old. How can you speed up your kids without resorting to the endless parroting of "Hurry up! Let's go! We're late!"?

Your Strategy

Plan ahead, don't push from behind.

What to Try First

Face facts: you're the only one who cares about getting out that door on time. In order to accomplish this, be realistic and start getting ready twenty minutes in advance instead of five.

The Practical Stuff

Make sure you lead the way by moving into action first. Don't stand over them urging them to "hurry up, hurry up." Tell them once and then put your coat on and open the door. Tell them you'll wait in the car. Someone waiting in a car has a surprising amount of pull on the person dawdling inside the house. These are all positive actions that let your kids know they are about to be left behind, putting the onus on them for a change. If it's a younger child, provide a choice: "Do you want to walk out or do you want me to carry you?"

If they're dawdling on purpose, inching along uncharacteristically, they are usually rebelling against being controlled by your constant nagging. Telling them to hurry up, therefore, just makes them go slower.

✓ Let them experience the consequence of their lateness: they miss swimming lessons; get booted off the hockey team; don't have time for a bedtime story; or get a detention at school.

✓ Tell them you are leaving in ten minutes, and stick to it so they know you are always serious about your deadlines.

✓ Give your kids a good sense of social duty, a big part of which is promptness. Show them how it's used to build social relationships: with their teacher; their friends; their hockey coach; their grandparents; and any other people they interact with.

✓ Establishing consistent routines can really help to reduce dawdling, particularly at bedtime and in the mornings — both prime dawdling times. See #33 (Late for School) for more tips.

KEY POINT Parents have to strike a balance between time and responsibility, and fun and exploration. Don't confuse dawdling with exploring. To kids, especially those under three years old, the voyage is always more important than the destination. Even as you are standing there fuming at the delay while your child examines a toad, you should realize that this is truly a wonderful state of mind that most adults have lost. In a kid's world, every little discovery is miraculous and their desire to explore should be encouraged.

To accommodate this, allow for a five-minute walk taking twenty minutes. Get into it. Bring a magnifying glass with you. Let your kids teach you something for a change.

2

BOSSINESS
Attila the Son

The Behaviour   Some people (you probably work for one) just love to boss everyone else around. They are usually at the centre of activity, but they don't get many dinner invitations. It's hard to watch your kid telling her friends what to do, arguing with them, and just generally trying to dominate everything in sight. No one likes to play with a kid who doesn't know how to give and take. Bossy kids tend to hang around younger children who are easier to control.

Why They Do It   The bossy kid feels weak and dominated. This is understandable; kids are surrounded by adults who are bigger and more competent than they are. Telling everyone else what to do — while conveniently forgetting how this might feel — is their way of overcoming their feelings of inadequacy.

Your Reaction   This kind of behaviour is not attractive, and it's hard to see it in your child. But it's really troublesome when they start to boss *you* around. How can we teach our kids to be assertive and strong without crossing the line into playground fascism?

Your Strategy   *Bossy kids feel significant by controlling others. Instead, let them earn that significance by being useful to others.*

What to Try First   Ignore them when they try to boss you around. Make them feel significant when they help in a positive way, by giving them a lot of attention and support.

The Practical Stuff

✓ Realize there is a silver lining in this cloud. Look for the many positive aspects of bossy kids, some of which are listed later in this chapter. For example, since they are so assertive, they are usually easy to talk to. They have ideas and energy. Take advantage of this by asking for their opinion when you have a problem.

✓ The family meeting is a great place for them to operate. We *want* their ideas and we want them to have power — but legitimate, helpful power. Ask for advice about, and help with, the younger kids ("Jimmy watches too much TV. How can we get him to play outside more?"). Let them know they are helpful by saying things like: "Now *that* is a good idea," "That would work," or "You're very creative."

✓ Encourage them to be helpful around the house by giving them important, adult-like jobs such as:

- setting the table (especially when company is coming over, so it feels special)
- helping serve at a party
- looking after younger kids
- washing the car

✓ Play cooperative games that stress give and take rather than competition.

✓ Role play with a bossy kid to teach him about other people's feelings, and to explore different ways to express his ideas. You play him while he plays his friend. Use the same hectoring tone he uses so he can hear what he sounds like. Ask him how it felt. Most kids are honest, and they learn fast.

Do's

✓ Do ask them to imagine how their friends might feel when they are being told how to do every little thing.

✓ Do teach them appropriate ways of stating their desires, while taking into account the feelings and desires of others. For example: "I want to play baseball. Do you?"

✓ Do encourage them with positive attention when they're not bossy.

Don'ts

✗ Don't try to stop the behaviour by giving them labels: "My God! Are you ever bossy!"

✗ Don't ever comply with their demands if they try to boss you around. They have to learn early on that this approach doesn't work.

On the Plus Side

Attributes of the Bossy Kid
- has strong leadership qualities
- knows what he wants and how to set goals
- doesn't worry unduly about what others think
- has natural problem-solving skills

Are You Looking in the Mirror?

If your kid is bossy, maybe he's learning it from the master — you. Ask yourself whether you boss your kids around. Do you use the old chestnut "Because I said so!" when you tell them to do something? Think of how many commands you give them in a day — and that's after they have been bossed around at school for six hours. No wonder they want to try their hand at it. Try to teach them how *not* to be bossy the same way you (inadvertently) taught them to be bossy — by example. One good approach is to ask your kids to do things for you the same way you would ask a good friend. After all, you can't boss your friends around.

Also, having a family based on a rigid hierarchy — with Dad as the boss and everyone else in a pecking order from Mom down to the goldfish — might reinforce the idea that being the boss is a desirable goal. A more egalitarian, democratic family, on the other hand, will foster cooperation.

3

TEMPER TANTRUMS
Junior Goes Ballistic

The Behaviour

A full-blown temper tantrum is an awesome sight. Screaming, yelling, throwing, and violent body contortions right out of *The Exorcist* make this the one misbehaviour that is almost impossible to ignore. The sound and fury follows you all over the house. Tantrums are like little tornados — they can spring up out of nowhere, last for as long as a couple of hours, and then disappear just as quickly. The frazzled parent is left pondering the age-old question: "What was all *that* about?"

Why They Do It

Tantrums can start in the first year of life but seem to reach their peak when the child is about three years old. This is the "Golden Age" of temper tantrums because the child is starting to stretch his muscles, so to speak. He is learning how to get what he wants and has noticed that throwing himself on the ground and shrieking for an hour seems to work. Normally the bosses of the house, the parents suddenly find the power shifting to their young child. If it happens in public — there's nothing like an audience of perfect strangers to bring out the thespian in children — the kid suddenly has *all* the cards.

Your Reaction

Tantrums can make any parent feel angry, exhausted, powerless, and even frightened. After all, your little child appears to have completely lost control. But have they really?

Your Strategy

Try to stay calm. Having your own tantrum won't help. Never give in or do anything they can see as their victory. When it's over, have them clean up any mess and get on with your life.

What to Try First

Since tantrums are about getting what you want, the worst thing you can do is let them get it. If it's over

a toy you won't buy them, whatever you do, don't buy them that toy. Give in once and they will begin every tantrum with the hope that this time they will win again. Even saying something like "I'll think about it" or "maybe" is tantamount to giving in. A much saner approach is to ask them to leave the room. If they won't go, *you* leave. If there's no audience, there's no payoff and, you hope, no more tantrums. Your child has to learn that there is a limit to what you will put up with, and if they are going to behave like that, they can't be with you until they stop.

The Practical Stuff

✓ If they start throwing or breaking things, hold them until they stop, or put them in their room. Take out anything you don't want broken, but they should learn that if they break something in their own room they are really hurting themselves. Don't say anything about it, but don't be in a hurry to replace it either. Give them a chance to experience the loss.

✓ Let's say they started the tantrum because you wanted them to hang up their coat. After the fireworks have died down, ask them nicely to hang up their coat. Don't do anything for them until the coat has been hung up. If they made a mess, have them clean it up, *but only when they are no longer angry*. This takes patience, but the key to successful parenting is consistency.

✓ If they decide to go over the top in the library or the mall, you can forget about reasoning with them. Pick them up (don't drag them) and remove them from the store. Take them to your car (if you took a bus or walked, take them to a nearby bench). You might have to wait in the car until they calm down. Then go right home. Believe it or not, kids like to go out with you, and being taken home is not what they had in mind when they went into tantrum mode.

Prevention

✓ Plan ahead. BIG TIP: Don't take them out or expect too much from them when they are tired (see **#45** on public tantrums).

✓ Have a family meeting and get everyone to agree on some basic rules, such as: "If you don't eat dinner, you don't get a snack" or "When we go to the store, you can spend your allowance, but don't ask us to buy you anything else." When kids know the rules, it's easier to enforce them.

✓ Teach them that the best solution to a problem is achieved through words and cooperation rather than force. Do this over and over again and they learn creative problem solving — a skill that will be invaluable to them when they grow up.

✓ Teach your kid to take no for an answer. The pampered child feels that she is entitled to anything she wants and should be able to use any means to get it.

Worst-Case Scenario

Here's how a typical tantrum gets started. You are having tuna casserole for dinner but your kid says he hates tuna and wants a can of SpaghettiOs instead. You say no and — BOOM — the tantrum begins. You've had a long day and you know that if you give in a peaceful dinner will ensue. You reach for the can opener and all is well. Until the *next* time. This approach is short-term smart, long-term stupid.

Best-Case Scenario

When the tuna casserole hits the fan, instead of giving in, remove the tantrum thrower from the kitchen. Insist he go to his room, or outside, or some place where his histrionics won't spoil everyone's dinner. Of course, everyone's dinner *will* be spoiled because a serious tantrum will fill the house. But eventually he will stop and — eventually — so will the tantrums. Honest.

Follow-Up

After the dust has settled, ask him: "The next time you take exception to the tuna casserole, what's a better way to let me know?"

4

SWEARING
"Please Pass the @#%! Milk"*

The Behaviour
It's a beautiful summer day in the backyard. The birds are chirping and the squirrels are gambolling in the sunshine. You are enjoying yourself when all of a sudden one of your little darlings lets out with a four-letter word that straightens your hair, bugs your eyes, and takes your breath away.

Why They Do It
They do *everything* they see and hear — that's how they learn.

Your Reaction
Like a thunderbolt, the thought hits you: "If she said it *here*, she could say it at *Grandma's!*" Words have power, as you have just found out. The question is, what does one do with a four-year-old that has the face of a cherub and the mouth of a longshoreman?

Your Strategy

Don't make a big deal about it or you will give them a hot button they can push whenever they want. Calmly explain that we don't say those kinds of words to people because it would hurt their feelings.

What to Try First (with Younger Kids)

When younger kids swear, it's because they are experimenting with language. They have come across these magic words that send adults through the roof. The first thing to do is avoid giving the words any more power than they already have.

Tell them once that it's definitely not okay to talk like that and then leave it. Ignore it completely the next time you hear it. It might happen a few more times, but if they don't get *any* reaction most kids forget about it.

If they persist, they are doing it to get attention. Either ask them to leave the room or leave the room

yourself (IMPORTANT: make sure you do this in a calm way). They can come back when they are ready to stop turning the air blue. This way they get no payoff. If they do it at someone else's house, take them home. That should nip it in the bud.

HELPFUL HINT You might also take a good hard look at your own language. Kids can learn this in the street, but they also might be repeating what you said the last time you hit your thumb with a hammer.

What to Try First (with Older Kids)

Let's face it: swearing is cool, at least to an older kid who wants desperately to fit into his peer group and sound like an "adult." It's hard to control what your kid does when he is away from you. As long as he doesn't do it around adults and young kids, there's not much you can do about it.

If older kids swear — especially if they swear at you — it's probably for revenge. This kid wants to hurt you. You have to talk to him, but not about the swearing. Find out why he is so angry with you. Remain calm and friendly and use active listening techniques (see #5 for listening tips). If you can get him to tell you "It's because you yell at me too much," consider yourself lucky, because now you can fix it. Say something like: "I'm glad you told me. Let's try and solve this." You would be amazed how powerful an apology from a parent can be. Next, take a good look at how you are treating your child. You might need outside counselling to work it out.

5

CHEATING
The Kid with the Two-Headed Coin

The Behaviour

Cheating on exams, cheating at games — this is the type of misbehaviour that *really* makes you cringe. It's a crime against honour more than anything else. And if they don't get caught for a while, the thrill of power that comes from getting away with it can become addictive.

Why They Do It

Some kids have to get ahead no matter what. They like to outsmart those in authority or their rivals, and they feel good when they pull something off. Cheating behaviour could also be rooted in low self-esteem — the child who doesn't think he can pass the test or win the game on his own may resort to "alternative means." Other kids who cheat are so overindulged that they like to take the easy way out. Or they may see others as suckers:

"I'll do less and get more and you won't even know."

Your Reaction

Disappointment tops the list of reactions to this one. There is a certain slyness in cheating that parents don't like to see in their child. You know that not only can cheating get them into trouble now, but cheating later in life can have ruinous social consequences, not to mention tax audits and big trouble in Vegas.

Your Strategy

Cheating is very much a secretive behaviour. Work on helping your kid become more open and less grasping.

What to Try First

If you catch your child cheating or hear about it from the teacher, don't threaten punishment or start to lecture. Try expressing your interest: "I see you were cheating. What happened?" If you want your kid to reveal something, act curious rather than angry. Ask open-ended questions, such as: "What kind of consequences do you think could result from cheating?" Point out a couple of consequences yourself: "If you cheat on your math test you might get a good mark, but you haven't learned anything, which means that in the long run you lose."

The Practical Stuff

The point of calmly talking to your kid about cheating is to find out why she did it. Maybe she will say: "Because I didn't know the answer and didn't want you to get mad." Your response could be: "I'm not angry, or at least I'll try not to get angry. Besides, bad grades are helpful because they let you know where you need to be working, and that's important." Stress working harder — learning for the sake of understanding. Teach her not to compare herself to others so much, but to go for personal improvement (which is something you can't cheat at), so she won't cheat out of fear of failure.

Do's

✓ Do ask yourself if you tend to act superior, always coming up with the right answer. Do you make a big deal about being number one? If you do, stop acting like the intellectual king of the mountain or you might drive your child to any lengths to emulate you. Make sure you don't compare your kids to their friends or siblings, which could make them too competitive.

✓ Do concentrate on their strengths. Be encouraging. Look at the good in every act they do (it's almost always there). Focus on their efforts, not their results.

✓ Do make sure you are not being too controlling with your kids. Don't belittle or exclude them. Encourage them to act and talk openly. Include them in discussions. Watch how you talk about high achievers.

Don'ts

✗ Don't always rush in to make things easy for them. Let them learn through experience that life is not easy, and that hard work is the only solution.

✗ Don't do a victory dance on the table every time you win, or act depressed when you lose.

The Lost Art of Being a Good Listener

The way to encourage your kids to talk (about cheating or anything else) is to be a good listener. Here's how to accomplish the rare skill of having a good conversation with a child:

- Try to overcome the overwhelming desire to hear your own mellifluous voice. Instead, remain silent and hear what your child has to say.
- Maintain good eye contact.
- Do encouraging things, like nodding your head. Throw in some "uh huhs" and "yeahs" every once in a while.
- Learn to summarize what you have just heard: "So you think we were being unfair when we sent you to bed in the middle of your program?" This is called reflective listening and lets the child know you are paying attention. Also, if you have misinterpreted the situation, they can correct you.

6

CRYING
Water Power

The Behaviour

The sound of your child crying can either tear your heart out or drive you nuts, depending on why they are crying and how much more than four hours' sleep you had the night before. Crying is one of the few weapons nature has given children, and it is a powerful one. For newborns, it's their *only* form of communication.

Why They Do It

Your child might be crying to tell you that she is hungry, or hurt, or frightened. On the other hand, some kids cry in order to teach you that they are special and must be handled with kid gloves. They use their tears to get sympathy or special treatment. You end up scrambling to satisfy them for fear of a heart-rending crying jag at the mall.

Your Reaction   You instinctively want to help, console, or cheer up a sobbing person. Crying hits us at such a visceral level that it's hard to react rationally when it's used as a misbehaviour.

Your Strategy   *Determine whether the crying is about something serious or just a plea for special treatment. If it's the latter, don't treat them as highly sensitive creatures by coddling them when they cry.*

What to Try First   Noted child psychologist Rudolf Dreikurs once called crying "water power." It *is* powerful, but you have to teach your kids not to abuse it. They abuse it when their cry is a demand to be pampered, or to avoid anything remotely unpleasant, and/or to get their own way. To nip it in the bud, stop responding to it.

The Practical Stuff   Here are five strategies to stop unnecessary (and we stress the word *unnecessary*) crying:

1. Learn to tell the difference between crying that requires a response from you ("I'm in some serious pain here — come and help me!") and water power. If they throw themselves, sobbing, on the bed, don't rush over with excessive soothing and comforting. Don't make a big fuss if a young child bumps her head or scrapes a knee. Young kids can learn to really milk a good cry if you let them.
2. Tell them it's difficult to talk to them when they are crying, but that you will be happy to

discuss it when they are feeling better. Just make sure you don't go overboard consoling them. It's a good idea to give them some time alone to pull themselves together. Don't let the tears change any rules or decisions that have been made — like bed times, chores, or consequences.

3. If you can stand it, separate yourself mentally when they start to cry. Just keep doing what you were doing, as if there wasn't an air raid siren going off beside your ear. When they stop — and only then — address the issue.

4. When your kid does stop crying and wants to talk about the problem, give your full attention.

5. Make your child independent. Don't always try to protect them or be their constant companion. Give them things to do alone: chores, helping younger kids, homework, etc. This gives them a greater feeling of competence.

KEY POINT If you respond to crying meant to elicit your attention, or to win a battle, or to be served, you're sunk.

7

TALKING TOO MUCH
The Blah Blah Blahs

The Behaviour   Like many positive impulses, the urge to express ourselves can be abused. The overly talkative child follows you around the house, demanding your attention with endless questions, anecdotes, and blow-by-blow descriptions of the latest kids' movie. Younger kids quickly learn that if they use the magical word "why," they will always get an adult's attention. Wholesome quests for knowledge turn into an annoying maze of pointless questions:

Child: Daddy, why do people burp?
Parent: Because they swallow too much air while they are eating, and burping helps get rid of it.
Child: Why do they do that?
Parent: Everyone swallows air while eating, but if you eat too fast you swallow too much.

Child: Why?
Parent: (Sighing) It just happens.
Child: Why?
Parent: (Looking at watch) Honey, I gotta run.
Child: Why?

And so on.

Why They Do It   They do it for attention — plain and simple. The truth is, a lot of kids only feel significant when somebody is paying attention to them. They want it so badly that even negative attention (like being told to "shut up!") is better than being ignored.

Your Reaction   You're trapped. You want to communicate with your kids and teach them about the world, but it's clear that your child has her own agenda — one that has little to do with curiosity.

Your Strategy   *Either remove them from the room or take yourself out of hearing range.*

What to Try First   This is where you walk the line between having your own rights and letting your kids know they can talk to you. It's okay that your child is an extrovert, but you have to maintain your own space. Just be upfront about it: If you are busy and they want to talk, tell them "I'm cooking now, but we'll talk later." If they keep talking, ignore it. If you can mentally withdraw, good for you. If not, leave the room. The idea here is to withhold the payoff — your attention — for the excessive talking. If you are talking to a friend and the child keeps interrupting, just keep right on talking, after first explaining: "I'd like to hear about it when I'm through talking to my friend." (Be sure to explain the strategy to your friend beforehand.)

The Practical Stuff

✓ One good way to let your child know you have heard enough for a while is to just touch him on the shoulder, or put your arm around him, while he's still talking. This acknowledges him without giving your full attention.

✓ If you suspect you're getting caught up in the endless question game, listen to see if they are thoughtful questions or just attention-seeking chatter. If they are nonsense queries, go do something else or leave the room — just make sure they don't get a payoff for this behaviour.

✓ However tempting it may be, don't tell them to shut up. And avoid discouraging nicknames, like "chatterbox" or "motormouth." Children will try to live up to their labels.

KEY POINT Don't think you have to be available every time your kid has a question or a comment. This only teaches them to be self-centred. Teach them to be patient. Encourage them when they ask good questions. Tell them how helpful they are when they find something to do themselves — like colouring or reading — while you are working in the same room.

8

LYING
"Cookie Monster Broke the Lamp! Honest!"

The Behaviour

Who broke this lamp? How many times have you asked a question like this, only to be bombarded by twenty minutes of the most pathetic lies you have ever heard, full of mythical creatures, mysterious strangers, and larcenous siblings?

Why They Do It

Kids lie to get out of trouble, to impress, and to manipulate.

Your Reaction

The parent on the receiving end of these lies worries that their kid will grow up to be dishonest. It irks them that they can't trust their own child. They know that if they can't get a truthful answer to something as simple as "who spilled the milk?" from a three-year-old, they will be in real trouble when they ask their teenager why the family car is upside down in the ditch. Lying has to be nipped in the bud. But why did it start and how do you stop it?

Your Strategy

Make your kids trust you no matter what they do. Help them find a solution to whatever problem they are lying about.

What to Try First

Try to get your kids to trust you enough so that they feel that every problem — from spilling the milk to breaking Grandma's Wedgwood bowl — can be worked out without severe punishment (which any intelligent being will try very hard to avoid).

The Practical Stuff

✓ First of all, let them know you love them no matter what they have done.

✓ Don't overreact (to the behaviour or the lie), and especially avoid shouts or threats.

✓ In a calm and friendly way, talk about the mistake. Be as understanding as you can.

✓ Give them a payoff for telling the truth by openly admiring their courage. They have to learn that the truth is more powerful than lying.

✓ Establish rules so the misbehaviour can be avoided in the future.

Anatomy of a Lie

Lying can begin early in life. Kids often lie about their age (they add a few years in a reversal of the common adult trend). Sometimes they lie to out-smart you, or (in a power struggle) simply to rebel. But usually it's to avoid catching hell for something they've done. To them, it's a creative form of problem solving. The more severe the expected punishment, the greater the chance they will fabricate a story in order to avoid trouble.

It's also important to distinguish between creative stories and outright falsehoods. While lying is usually an attempt to avoid trouble, the goal of the storyteller is to get attention.

Do's

✓ Do include your kids in looking for cooperative solutions to problems, rather than concentrating on punishment. If you come from the kind of family where every "bad" act (including spilling the milk) needs a fitting punishment, then chances are your kid will lie in self-defence.

✓ Do make it easy for them to tell the truth, but not too easy. If they are lying because they did something bad, tell them: "I'm glad you finally told me the truth, but it upsets me to hear about what you did." At this point they have to fix whatever happened — by restitution, or apologies, or whatever is required.

Don'ts

✗ Don't play detective: "All right! Which one of you reprobates broke my CD player?" Instead, say something like: "I see the CD player is broken" or "I see you broke the CD player. Do you want to talk about it?" It's hard to do this calmly, but the good news is, if you can learn how, you will have to do it less and less.

✗ Don't call your kid a liar. Kids often internalize this kind of verbal slap-in-the-face and begin to see themselves as liars. This will increase the likelihood that the behaviour will reoccur. Instead, learn to separate the doer from the deed — there's no need to get personal about these things.

9

RISK-TAKING
"Look Ma! No Brains!"

The Behaviour   Climbing a tree is one of the true joys of childhood. Climbing a really tall tree all the way to the
top, where a fall could kill you, is not. Parents with
thrill-seeking kids spend a lot of time with their
hearts in their throats as they watch their dare-
devil spawn dodge cars, run over rooftops, and ride
their bike down Dead Man's Hill with no hands.
Risk-taking can border on a death wish, as when
they taunt bigger and meaner kids just for the kick
of being chased by Butch, the school psychopath.
These kids play with fire — literally — and can
start shoplifting things just for the hell of it. To
their friends they're Indiana Jones. To their parents
they're another trip to the emergency room.

Why They Do It   Either to impress their friends, to get attention, or to break the bonds of overprotective parents.

Your Reaction   Fear, dread, hysteria — take your pick.

Your Strategy   *Remove them from the situation with a minimum of talk and attention. If it's not life threatening, let them get a few bumps and bruises.*

What to Try First   If he's done it before, it's a waste of breath to tell a kid that jumping off the roof or going down the slide upside down is dangerous. He already knows that. There are only two things you can do:

1. Take him inside and say in a firm, calm voice (without lecturing) that he can't play on the swing if he does something dangerous like wrap the chain around his neck. If he continues to act crazy on the swing, tell him that you will now have to supervise him. Since you can't supervise him outside, he has to come in until he promises to use the swing safely — let him decide when he's ready. If you see he isn't keeping his word, you decide when he can go back out.
2. If it's not life threatening or it won't cause lasting harm, let him get a little bruised. This is hard for a parent to do, but if the circumstances are right, it is very effective. Pain is a wonderful teacher for stubborn kids like this.

The Three Types of Risk-Taker

Besides the obvious adrenalin rush, kids take risks in order to get attention and respect. Risk-takers fall into three basic types:

1. **The Thrill Seeker.** This kid loves the challenge and the unknown aspect of jumping off a cliff. He might be overprotected by his parents, so he has not yet learned that life is dangerous. He hasn't been allowed his full share of bumps and bruises like the average kid. He walks out in the street like he was taking a stroll through heaven. Solution: Without letting him get run over by a car, let him experience just how dangerous life can be if you're not careful. For example, let him smack into the wall if he insists on riding his pogo stick with his eyes closed.

2. **The Contrarian.** She gets her kicks from defying her parents, who usually overreact to her stunts. She stands up on a table and they run after her hysterically with a net. Solution: Don't respond when she pushes your buttons. If you do have to intervene (for instance, to save her life) do it as nonchalantly as possible so she can't possibly get a payoff.

3. **The Superhero.** He wants to impress his friends with his courage and death-defying bravado. Solution: You can't control what he does when he's with other kids. Your best bet is prevention (see below).

The Practical Stuff

✓ Don't be so overprotective. If they go for a walk with you and don't watch where they're going, let them trip over a rock and land in the mud. You're only being mean if you laugh. Besides, kids can live with a barked shin. They have to learn to watch out for themselves because you can't be their guardian angel forever.

✓ Try not to nag. Telling them that they are going to "trip with that stick and poke someone's eye out while breaking your neck" is futile after the tenth time. Instead, make a firm rule about not running with sticks. Demonstrate a firmness and consistency about safety rules. For instance, if you go out for a family walk and they keep darting into the street, make them hold your hand until they tell you they're ready to stay on the sidewalk.

✓ Have them take care of a pet. Being responsible for Fluffy's safety will make them more aware of danger.

✓ Let them look after younger children. This will also foster caution and awareness.

✓ If they do hurt themselves, let them clean it and put the bandage on. This not only helps them keep their pride, but deprives them of the payoff of attention. Whatever you do, don't ever say things like "Ahh, poor you" or "Told ya!"

✓ Give this kind of kid more supervision than you would to a more cautious child.

10

STEALING
She's Gotta Have It

The Behaviour   You probably think this is how Al Capone got started. A lot of kids dabble in it, but stealing is one childhood misbehaviour that is guaranteed to send parents looking for a big stick.

Why They Do It   Sometimes kids take what is not theirs just because they want it and are accustomed to instantly getting what they want. Sometimes they steal to impress their friends with their damn-the-consequences bravado and their generous sharing of the loot. They can even steal *from* their friends. Other times they do it to get back at their parents.

Your Reaction   Having a tiny criminal in the family is a real heartbreaker. For some parents it's hard to say what's worse, the actual stealing or the pitifully transparent lies that go along with this most petty of crimes.

Your Strategy

Don't pamper them or they will feel they are entitled to everything they crave. Do give them an allowance so they can satisfy reasonable desires.

What to Try First

The best way to stop your child from stealing is to prevent it from happening in the first place. There are three ways to pull this off:

1. Don't overindulge them.
2. Give them a strong sense of right and wrong.
3. Teach them to have social interest so that they care about how their actions affect others.

The Practical Stuff

✓ They say the road to hell is paved with good intentions — when you hear this, think of overindulgence, or pampering (see **#44** on The Gimmes). The overindulgent parent wants what we all want: happy children. But they try to achieve it by giving their child everything they ask for. Ironically, this results in profoundly unhappy kids. For one thing, the reality is that you can't have everything in life, and pampered people have trouble dealing with this. Worse, when someone does say no, an overindulged kid's first impulse is to simply take it. That's because the pampered child feels entitled. Start them out this way and you pay the price later, as that hot package of 25¢ candy becomes a $150 video game.

Instead, decide what is reasonable for your child to have and then be firm about it. If you decide to buy them candy once a week, stick to it no matter what kind of Academy Award–class begging goes on. If you say no only occasionally, they think you're just being mean. It would help if they don't see you weaken and buy on impulse yourself.

✓ Give them an allowance. Stealing can be seen as an ingenious (but reprehensible) way for a young child to get what they want. Giving them an allowance provides an alternative to pampering. If they spend it fast, don't cave in and buy them something anyway. No overdrafts!

✓ *HELPFUL HINT* If they are really easy to catch, revenge is probably the prime motivation. Sometimes kids steal for spite. For kids who are really angry at their parents, stealing is a great way to get back at them. Not only do they get a spiffy new toy, but they drag their cold-hearted folks through hell at the same time.

Before you hit the roof, understand that children who want to hurt you feel hurt themselves. Now is the time to talk to them about their feelings, something parents — who like to lay down the law hard and fast — don't do often enough. The result is that our kids often don't learn to communicate what they are thinking and feeling. And communication is the forerunner to problem solving.

✓ Sometimes a really good kid will steal because of peer pressure. This problem needs a lot of communication. You can't be with her all the time, so you'll have to show your child how to resist conforming when the crowd is being stupid. Try using role play: you be her and she can play her friends planning the big heist. Then reverse it. Try to have some fun with it. This method can also be used in later years when smoking and drinking become an issue.

✓ The next step is to help your child develop social interest (caring about others) and a strong sense of values. The best way to do this is to get your child involved in charitable and helpful activities:

- Collecting used toys for needy children
- Running errands for the elderly
- Volunteering at a food bank
- Looking after younger kids while you're making dinner

✓ More supervision is probably a good idea. Kids who roam around, bored and unfocused, can turn to the thrill of being bad. Keep them busy with wholesome (but fun) stuff like sports, games, books they will actually read, Cubs, Brownies, organized teams, and science clubs.

✓ Ask them how they would feel if someone took something from them. Get them to stand in other people's shoes. Tell them what you think is right or wrong. And don't short-change the system yourself — if they see you lying about their age so they can get into the zoo for free, why *shouldn't* they steal?

What to Do When the Phone Call Comes

Your first reaction — yelling, hitting, punishing — is not the best way, no matter how good it makes you feel. You can show your outrage at this antisocial act, but punishment doesn't work. Restitution is the answer. The child has to take responsibility and make things right. This will involve returning stolen property (or paying for the candy they ate), and an apology to the victim. Go with them when they do this. Some store owners will bar your kid — this is good because it's a great consequence.

11

SULKING
The Silent Anger

The Behaviour A good sulk can fill the house with black waves of anger. A good sulker can make it last for days, until even the *kid* doesn't remember what started it. Usually though, it's because somebody said the "N" word — NO! You didn't let them have a sleepover with twelve of their friends, or buy another toy, or watch *The Texas Chain Saw Massacre*.

Why They Do It A sulk is nothing more than a silent temper tantrum. This kid feels entitled to something she didn't get, and she's angry. Her response — the silent treatment.

Your Reaction Your first impulse with a sulking kid is to try to make them happy. They're sitting there with their arms clenched tightly to their body, looking like they've got six lemons in their mouth. You want to say: "Ahhh, what's the matter honey?" A host of subtle feelings are aroused in the parents of sulking children, with guilt predominating, followed closely by a growing desire to give in. Sulking is so effective, in fact, that after a while most parents would welcome a good, old-fashioned temper tantrum.

Your Strategy

Ignore it. Then get them to talk about it.

What to Try First

Don't give in. First of all, remind yourself that they started sulking because you refused a request. Sulking is an aggressive withdrawal — an attempt to manipulate. It's natural to want things and, intelligent creatures that they are, children will use sulking over and over again if it helps them get what they want even once. If you ignore it, there's no payoff.

HELPFUL HINT If they keep on sulking, you know they're getting some kind of payoff.

The Practical Stuff

✓ Don't act like you are upset by the sulking. Don't change any of your activities or do anything differently. Keep your body language normal and your attitude cheerful, or at least neutral.

✓ If it gets too obnoxious, ask them to leave the room.

✓ After the sulk is over, encourage them to talk. This kid needs to know that you want to understand their feelings about the problem.

KEY POINT The most important thing is to eventually get them talking about disappointments and how they should be handled.

Do's

✓ Do keep in mind that your child may have a legitimate beef. Don't automatically dismiss their demands or concerns. The difference between a knapsack and a gym bag may seem trivial to you, but it can make or break your child's day. Let your kids know you are always willing to talk about their problems. Provide alternatives to sulking.

✓ Do nip it in the bud. Before they go into a sulk, say something like: "You look upset. Do you want to talk about it?" If they don't, let it go.

✓ Do encourage them if they eventually start talking about the problem by saying: "I like it when you talk about things even though you are upset."

Don'ts

✗ Don't pander to the sulk or try to snap them out of it by asking if they want to watch the baseball game or have a hot chocolate — that's a payoff.

✗ Don't act as a negative role model by sulking yourself, or giving your spouse the cold shoulder.

✗ Don't put up with it. Someone in full sulk can

stink up a room better than week-old fish. It's the height of passive aggression. When it gets too obnoxious, ask them to leave. If it's a rebellious older child, you may have to leave the room yourself. But make sure you do it without anger. Without an audience, most kids will not bother to waste a good performance.

ANOTHER KEY POINT Remember, they are not being devious — they really are unhappy. But don't make the mistake of thinking that your job is to keep your child perpetually happy. A sulking child often has a parent who feels sorry for them. The child soon realizes that their unhappiness is a powerful tool.

12

TALKING BACK
Out of the Big Mouth of Babes

The Behaviour   You would think that for all you do as a parent, the least you could ask for is a little respect. Talking back is one of the most potent forms of disrespect a child can inflict on a parent. They may not be able to swim yet, or drive a car, but boy do they know how to use their verbal skills to get your goat. Sarcasm ("Oh boy. Meat loaf again. Yum Yum!"), invective ("I hate you!"), rhetorical questions ("What are you — deaf?"), and everyone's favourite, derisive repetition ("Yeah, yeah, yeah"), are used with the panache and skill of Shakespeare. This is especially fun when you have company.

Why They Do It   In a word — revenge!

Your Reaction   If an adult talked to you this way, you would simply refuse to have anything further to do with them. But when your kids do it, it's hard not to respond in kind. Your family life starts to resemble something out of *Who's Afraid of Virginia Woolf?* How can you stop this most embarrassing of misbehaviours while maintaining your civility?

Your Strategy

If your kids talk back to you, ask yourself how you talk to them. Maybe the first step is to clean up your own act.

What to Try First

Figure out if you are either pampering or verbally razing your kids. Think about it. Young kids model most of their behaviour after their parents. If they're verbally abusing you, they're certainly not getting it from watching reruns of *The Dick Van Dyke Show*.

You might also be pampering your kids so much they feel they're the boss. They see you as someone who is less than equal and therefore doesn't deserve respect.

The solution is to teach your kids that in life they can't have everything, and that everyone should be treated with respect. You can say something like: "I know you don't want to do this but it must be done anyway." This at least acknowledges their feelings.

The Practical Stuff

✓ Take some responsibility for the behaviour yourself. Do you constantly:

- nag — "I'm getting sick and tired of telling you how sick and tired I am of . . ."

- call people names — "Boy, are you ever sloppy."
- pontificate — "If you had a modicum of brains you would realize . . ."
- dominate — "Because I said so, that's why!"
- act pushy — "Come on, come on! Hurry up!"

✓ Resolve to talk to your kids the same way you would talk to any adult you are friendly with.

✓ If they verbally abuse you, leave the room. Lock yourself in the bathroom with a good book if you have to, or even go for a drive if it's an older child. For a younger child, ask them to leave the room and not come back until they can act respectfully. If they won't go, remove them yourself. Don't get upset or they will win.

✓ Sometimes they don't realize they've gone over the top. Make them stop and think about their behaviour by saying things like "I don't like being called that" or "Do you think what you just said to me is all right?" Above all, let them know that talking back won't get them what they want.

✓ Use reflective listening when they talk back (see #5 for tips). Here are two scenarios:

Scenario A

Parent: Dammit! I've told you five times to get to bed. It's like talking to a brick wall.

Kid: I hate you! I don't want to go to bed!

Parent: Don't talk to me that way. I'm your mother.

Kid: Don't remind me.

Parent: Okay. That does it. No more TV for you for a week.

Scenario B

Parent: It's time for bed. What are you still doing up?

Kid: But I don't want to go to bed. It's not fair.

Parent: I'm glad you told me. I didn't know you felt that way. (This usually stops them in their tracks.)

Kid: (still upset but on unsteady ground) It really isn't fair.

Parent: It sounds like you really don't like it when I keep telling you to go to bed.

Kid: Yeah.

Parent: Maybe you and I should sit down and figure out what is the best time for you to go to sleep?

This is a good example of healthy conflict resolution that helps, rather than hurts, the relationship. You use it to show the child you are listening, and also to explain, in a non-manipulative way, what you think is happening.

13

WHINING
The Ultimate Irritant

The Behaviour   Your child whines from the moment he wakes up until he falls asleep. Over and over again he moans: "I want a glass of juuuuice. Pleeease, mommy, I want it NOOOOW!" or "I don't like *this* dinner, I want a *new* dinner."

Why They Do It   It works.

Your Reaction   Both the tone and the relentless repetition of whining can drive a parent batty. It's like having a mosquito trapped in your head. Kids instinctively know this, so whining can quickly become a major weapon in the parent–child power struggle.

Your Strategy   *Never give in to a whining request.*

What to Try First

As with any other annoying noise, your first impulse is to hit the "off switch" — to give him whatever he is whining for. But by giving in you let him achieve both his goals (attention and service). Total victory! Unless you want offspring who are still whining in their 40s, don't do it.

The Practical Stuff

Four Ways to Avoid Giving In:

1. Ignore the whining. Sure it's difficult, but never *ever* respond to a whining request. Act busy. Pretend you don't hear it. This works particularly well for attention seekers.
2. Give him a choice: "I'd be happy to get you a sandwich if you ask in a nice way."
3. Do the unexpected. Walk into the room with a bright, cheerful "Good morning honey!" instead of the usual "Jonathan, for crying out loud, stop whining!" This should stun him into at least a temporary silence.
4. Leave the room. This deprives him of the object of his whining — which is you. You can come back when the whining stops. If you are at the mall, take him home. The pet shop, New York Fries, and Toys "R" Us will have to wait.

Prevention

The trick to preventing future whining is to consistently reinforce good behaviour. When he asks in a nice way, let him know it's appreciated: "Gee. I really like it when you ask nicely." Also, stop reacting with exasperated whines of your own: "You're driving me crazy!" or "My God, that's obnoxious!" This not only adds to the general noise, but it lowers your child's self-esteem by making him think of himself as a bad person.

Above all, watch for opportunities throughout the day to teach your child to be independent. He can dress himself and get his own snacks if they are placed in an accessible cupboard. With a step stool, he can get himself a drink of water. His juice can be placed in a small pitcher on a low shelf in the fridge. Sure, it's easier to pour the juice yourself than it is to clean up the inevitable spill. But that would discourage your child's natural drive for independence. Take comfort in the fact that the more he is encouraged to do for himself, the less he will whine.

HELPFUL HINT Have a cozy little *tête-à-tête* (after everyone has calmed down) so you can explain that you simply don't respond to whining. Lay out exactly what you will and won't do if he whines. It's up to you to teach him civilized alternatives.

14

TOO MUCH TV
Beaching the Channel Surfers

The Behaviour   Television is seductive for adults, and this goes
double for kids. Flip it on and watch them turn
into wide-eyed little zombies. They don't play.
They don't interact. They don't do anything but
stare at the screen watching mindless cartoons, ads
for this year's toy, and the same movie 400 times in
a row. It's even worse when they stumble upon a
program that is so adult it would make *you* blush.
The only good thing is that when kids watch TV,
they're *quiet* — a blissful state so rare that it tempts
us to use television as an electronic baby sitter
more than we would like to admit.

Why They Do It   Are you kidding?

Your Reaction

You are worried that your kids are watching too much TV and missing out on more creative pursuits, like drawing and reading. You also object to the persuasive consumerism that works all too well on children. You would like to cut down and control what they watch, but how can you try to regulate an activity you like to indulge in yourself? As in many homes, the TV, rather than the family, has become the centre of your universe.

Your Strategy

Teach older kids why some programs are good to watch and some are harmful. Then decide together what and how much they should watch. For younger kids (five and under), limit and control their TV viewing.

What to Try First

The first thing to do is accept the TV — but not passively. Sit down with them and watch what they view. Control your natural urge to lay down the law and censor everything. Realize that your kids are tenacious and will see a forbidden program somewhere else if they put their mind to it.

You will have to prescreen programs for children under five years old. Use the VCR — one of the modern inventions that actually does improve life — so you can judge a program's appropriateness before you let your kids watch it. Keep lots of suitable movies on hand, and don't let young kids watch the (often violent) news. If you can afford it, get a channel that has only family-oriented programming without commercials.

The Practical Stuff

✓ Don't leave the TV on all day, especially if no one is watching it. Otherwise it may become omnipresent, like very loud wallpaper. Make watching TV a special occurrence.

✓ Go through the *TV Guide* with them and use a highlighter to mark programs everyone agrees upon. Turn the TV off as soon as the show is over.

✓ The best way to combat violence on TV is to make sure your kids come from a loving home where there is no real physical or verbal abuse. You can also encourage your kids to write letters to TV stations to protest the amount of violence they see.

✓ Plan a bunch of interesting family activities that don't involve the TV. This is going to take more than a few *National Geographic*s and a *Monopoly* game. TV is mesmerizing, so you'll need to be just as creative to compete with it. Here are some tips on how to beat the tube at its own game:

- Schedule one or two nights a week for family fun. Don't worry if this isn't exactly spine-tingling drama; most kids would rather play *Pictionary* with you than watch a cartoon cat and mouse hurt each other. All it takes is your time — something that is often in short supply — but when it comes to weaning your kids off the tube, you are the best alternative.
- Buy lots of games and make sure your house is stocked with books — even talking books on tape (check out your local library). Set up a play house. Teach them how to play charades (don't roll your eyes — kids love it).
- Encourage them to invite friends over, and let *them* do the entertaining.
- Ham it up — form a family band or stage some simple plays. Sure it's a lot of work, but you can relax with the *Tonight Show* after the kids are in bed.

Sex and Violence

Now that we have your attention, let's look at two of TV's most popular programming features.

When faced with sex and violence on TV, your first impulse as a parent is to get what is euphemistically called a "V" chip — a device that blocks the reception of violent programs. This is both good and bad. The chip gives you a lot more control over what your kids watch, and allows you to eliminate the truly dangerous. The drawback is that you also want to teach them how to discriminate between good TV and bad TV — to get them to take the responsibility.

Besides, they will see this stuff in other places.

Watch TV with your kids. Teach them how to deal with violent images by asking them questions like:

- Do you think it was right what they did to each other?
- How else could they have solved the problem?
- Do you think people who hit each other like that could really walk away from it?
- Why do you think so many of these shows have people with guns?
- Do you really think you should watch this?

HELPFUL HINT Take your kids to the taping of a real TV show so they can better understand the medium.

A MATTER
OF HABITS

1š

PERSONAL HYGIENE
The Fungus Among Us

The Behaviour   Most kids couldn't care less about personal hygiene. That comes later, with the rush of hormones. Until then, they can walk around with some kind of thick, crusty rime on every exposed surface without a worry in the world. Teeth go green, hair goes lank, and clothes take on a life of their own.

Why They Do It   It's a lot more fun to play in the mud with your friends than to take it off in the bathtub. For most kids, personal hygiene is low on the priority list, down there with other adult concerns like being on time and saving money. If you are constantly nagging them about it, their reaction could be to simply dig in their heels. And of course the older they get, the more likely it is that poor hygiene is a case of rebellion, especially if you are a "neat freak."

Your Reaction	The word "effluvia" begins to show up in your thoughts. You worry that your kid's health will suffer — whether from cavities or the plague. You also wonder if this will reflect badly on you as a parent.
Your Strategy	*Relax. If it's not a pattern, just make bathing and grooming more fun. If the kid wants to be dirty, it's a power struggle. Explain the social consequences.*
What to Try First	Stop worrying about what other people will think. This is easier said than done, but you have to divorce your "pig pen" kid from your own pride. Your kid's choices are not a reflection on you. At the very least this will automatically eliminate the power struggle factor.

Next, pediatricians say that when it comes to healthy hygiene, it is good enough to bath once a week. The important thing is to establish good routines so kids get clean without thinking about it — and without a power struggle. |
| **The Practical Stuff** | ✓ Make it fun. Use self-cleaning bubble bath and stock up on fun bath toys. Often kids are tired after dinner — too tired to take a bath without a fight — so surprise them occasionally with a Saturday afternoon bath. Play some music and do anything else you can think of to make it seem like a special occasion.

✓ Educate them. Use picture books to explain about germs. Get a doctor or a nurse or a dentist to explain it. |

✓ Some kids hate strong physical sensations. Be very gentle with kids like this. Use non-stinging shampoo and a rolled-up washcloth to shield their eyes from the soap. Get them to wash and brush their doll's hair. This lets them act out an unpleasant experience on the doll, and to — over time — come to accept it.

✓ Use an egg timer when they brush their teeth so they know how long to keep at it.

✓ Brush their hair while it's still wet. It hurts more if it has time to dry snarled. Use conditioner.

✓ Appeal to their vanity — it sure works on adults. Let them know what a knockout they are when they smell fresh and have gleaming teeth and lustrous hair.

✓ Brush your teeth with them. This works especially well for those under five years old, who like the company and like to model what you do.

Consequences   If all of the above fail, don't get upset, yell, belittle, whine, wheedle, or brush anyone's teeth against their will. Do, however, try the following natural and logical consequences:

- Tell them that if they don't brush their teeth they will get cavities. Get your dentist to show them a picture of a rotten tooth. Then, welcome a cavity. You've warned them and when your prediction comes true, it strengthens your authority. Ration their sugar intake until they start to take better care of their teeth. Have older kids use their allowance to pay part of the dentist bill. Make sure they know this is a direct result of their actions, not just a punishment. After all, why should you be stuck with a big dentist bill while your kid is whooping it up with a bag of gummie bears?
- Point out some of the obvious social consequences of things like bad breath and body odour.
- If their clothes are truly filthy, don't let them sit on the furniture. Tell them you can't take them on outings because they offend everyone. Give them a choice between coming clean and getting a sitter.

16

BAD HABITS
"Put That Back in Your Nose Where It Belongs!"

The Behaviour   Thumbsucking, nosepicking, nailbiting, hairsucking, skinpicking — raising kids is not pretty. They develop nasty habits that are hard to break.

Why They Do It   They start doing it because they like it. Sucking a thumb can be soothing, nailbiting can release tension, and that stuff in your nose has got to come out somehow. You can assume a lot of this behaviour is not done to aggravate you or gross you out, unless you try so hard to correct it that it becomes the focus of a power struggle. Even when it is done with a particular goal in mind, the goal is usually unconscious.

Your Reaction   You wonder what walking around with a thumb in their mouth will do to their social life, not to mention their teeth. And nailbiters look so nervous and neurotic — is that your fault? Some misbehaviour can make you angry, but seeing your child with his finger buried in his nose up to the second knuckle just makes you kind of queasy. How can you get him to stop?

Your Strategy

No matter how gross it is, be cool about their bad habits. Making a big deal about it will just prolong the behaviour.

What to Try First

Don't worry so much about the cause — if the first thing they saw upon exiting the birth canal was Dad anxiously biting *his* nails, that's water under the bridge by now. Instead, give them some good reasons to stop. Tell them that sucking their thumb, for example, is not a good idea because:

- It doesn't look nice
- They could get teased
- It will give them buck teeth

HELPFUL HINT Don't insult them by telling them they "look like a baby." And don't overdo all those great reasons to stop. If you do, you can bet the behaviour will change from a mere habit to a weapon in the struggle for either power or attention.

Remember, bad habits are intensified by nagging. If your kid is into power and you keep telling her not to suck her hair, you can be sure she's going to suck her hair. If she wants attention, a finger up the

nose will be the easiest way to get it. Besides, you can usually rely on peer pressure to accomplish what a thousand hours of nagging will not. In other words, once your child starts going to school, the ribbing she takes about her thumbsucking and nosepicking should end it fast enough.

The Practical Stuff

✓ Don't talk to them or pay attention to them when they suck their thumb (or bite their nails or pick their nose). Start talking as soon as that thumb comes out.

✓ If it really bothers you, ask them to leave the room. Let them know that bad habits are gross (don't ever tell a child that *she's* gross) and disrespectful of other people. They can come back when they stop.

✓ When they are four or five years old, you can talk to them about how they could stop. Say something like: "I know it's hard for you to stop. Let's see what we can come up with to help you." If the kid is into it, try some deterrents, like balls that can be put on the thumb, or foul-tasting liquids (see your doctor) that can be painted on thumbs and nails. BIG TIP: A lot of girls will stop biting their nails if you let them wear nail polish.

17

BATHROOM PROBLEMS
Poop and Circumstance

The Behaviour   Going to the bathroom in your *pants*! How's that for misbehaviour? After carefully and successfully (you thought) toilet training your child, they suddenly start walking funny and smelling a little high. Even worse, some kids do it in strange places like behind the couch — an Easter Egg Hunt to remember. This can get very creative, as when boys take great joy in peeing down the stairs. And it can happen at any age. Even ten-year-olds can do it. Your kid knows how to relieve himself in the proper way, but for some reason isn't doing it.

Why They Do It   Toilet terrorism is about power. Essentially, letting go in your shorts is a form of rebellion. The kid is saying: "I'll go where *I* want." They are also saying: "I won't stop having fun to go to the bathroom." One is rebellion against you, the other against the demands of life. Of course, if it persists you should see a doctor in order to rule out a physical cause.

Your Reaction

You start to dread his approach, and he's not exactly becoming a popular guy with his friends either. As a parent it's not only gross, it's embarrassing. You can't help but feel badly when the teacher calls asking you to pick up your child and hose him down. You feel angry and frustrated and somehow responsible. This is one misbehaviour you would *love* to correct.

Your Strategy

Believe it or not, the best solution is to simply relax with it and leave it up to them.

What to Try First

Absolutely nothing, because what you don't want to do is make it worse or last longer than it has to. Time will solve this problem — after all, twenty-year-olds don't do it. But if you've opened one too many of those ripe little surprise packages, here are some tips on how to get your child through this stinky phase more quickly.

The Practical Stuff

✓ Create an Accident Kit (for kids four-and-a-half years old and up). Tell them: "Accidents sometimes happen. I'll show you how to clean it up." The kit could include a bucket for their dirty pants, as well as a wet washcloth, soap, and a towel. Once they are clean, they can dress themselves. Assist as little as possible, but with younger kids you will have to help. Make it brisk and business-like, not a fun game with a lot of banter.

✓ Give them consequences if they won't clean up by themselves. Remind them that people don't like to be around that kind of smell. Ask them to wait in the bathroom until they're ready to clean up. Leave some toys in there for them.

Do's

✓ Do let them know you love them anyway. Make encouraging statements about how you know they can overcome this.

Don'ts

✗ Don't make a big deal about it if they do go in the right place. Show a quiet confidence.

✗ Don't overreact. If you try to force them to go where you want them to, you are joining in the power struggle — round one to the kid. Instead, see this in the same light as other, less pungent, misbehaviour.

✗ Don't talk about it incessantly or lecture them. Kids are brilliant — they already *know* dumping in their pants is wrong. Never explain to a kid something he already knows.

✗ Don't expect this to change overnight. It could take (sorry about this) three to six months, depending on how well you handle it. And remember, it can happen occasionally as an accident, or it can be situational, but if they do it every day they are pushing your buttons.

✗ Don't reward them with money when they do manage to hit the bowl. We know of one case where a child stopped the inappropriate behaviour for a month and saved up enough to buy a $30 radio, only to start again.

18

CLOTHES ENCOUNTERS
"You're Going to Wear That?"

The Behaviour The trouble starts when parents and kids have different ideas of what clothing is acceptable. A child may have one kind of outfit they will wear — maybe it's jeans and a T-shirt, or leggings and a baggy sweater — and refuse to even consider anything else. This doesn't sit well with parents who have bought a closet full of other kinds of clothes they wish their kids would wear. Some kids simply won't dress appropriately — either they are dedicated slobs who would rather die than wear nice clothes to Grandma's on Sunday, or they are "super femmes" who insist on wearing a frilly dress to the playground. And then there is the most common of all clothing rebels, the child who refuses to wear a warm coat to school on sub-zero days. Of course these clothing wars happen at the most stressful of times: when they're late for school or you're getting ready to go out.

Why They Do It   Choosing what clothes to wear is about as personal as it gets. It's only natural that people (yes, three-year-olds are people too) want to express their individuality, or their affiliation with a social group, through their clothing. Arguing about clothes is about having some control over your life. Besides, most kids, especially boys, hate getting dressed up. They are too active to enjoy restrictive clothes and resent having to wear something no self-respecting cowboy would be caught dead in.

Your Reaction   It's almost impossible for parents to refrain from telling their kids what to wear. Trying to get your kids to dress as you think they should is a thankless task, as irresistible as it is hopeless.

Your Strategy   *What they wear should be left up to them. If it's inappropriate, let them suffer the consequences. Above all, give them a choice.*

What to Try First   Give them the information and then get out of the way. Seven- or eight-year-olds can make a lot of their own choices. Your job is to teach them how to make *good* choices. Include them in discussions about what to wear. Ask them what they think they should wear if the temperature is ten below. If they watch you get dressed, say something like: "Yep, it sure is going to be cold today. Better wear my sweater." This gives them cues, rather than orders.

The Practical Stuff

✓ Teach your kids how to read a thermometer or the weather forecast in the morning paper. Point out what could happen if they wear a T-shirt and shorts in a blizzard. Then hope they actually do suffer a consequence — not severe enough to injure them, but bad enough to make them trust you (and the thermometer) more in the future. Start this in the fall before the weather gets serious. You can nudge them in the right direction by stocking their dresser with only winter clothes during that season.

✓ Teach them how to coordinate different tops and bottoms when you are shopping with them.

✓ For kids who are sensitive about the feel of things — the Princess and the Pea syndrome — watch out for scratchy fabrics, tight fits, or items that rub or irritate.

✓ Today's dress codes are very relaxed, but if having the kids dressed up for a special occasion is really important to you, you may have to plan ahead. Book a sitter — if the kid won't dress up, she can't come. She won't like this and neither will you, but you should only have to resort to this once. On the positive side, this will teach her that life has social requirements to which she must sometimes conform.

HELPFUL HINT Often their rigid wardrobe preference is just a stage. It probably won't last long unless you make a big deal about it.

Do's

✓ Do realize that you have a lot of influence, but only if you're subtle. For example, take the fussy child with you when you shop for clothes. In a friendly way, encourage them to try on different things.

✓ Do stock up on leggings and sweat shirts if that's all they will wear, and forget about dresses or jeans for a while.

✓ Do make your child responsible for washing the one item of clothing he *will* wear. If his approach to personal hygiene is somewhat relaxed, point out how smelling like a derelict can affect his social life.

Don'ts

✗ Don't get into power struggles over clothes. It's a battle you can't win and, in most cases, shouldn't even be fighting.

✗ Don't let everyone make a fuss ("Ooooh! Doesn't she look sweet!") if you don't want your daughter to fixate on frilly dresses.

✗ Don't foist your dressing style on them. Realize that they know a lot more about what's hip in their social circle than you do. How would you like it if your kids made you go to work in a purple Barney outfit?

The Younger Child

Obviously, you have to give some sartorial guidance to a two- or three-year-old. The trick here is to give them a choice so they feel they have some control over their lives. Lay out two or three outfits for them — not so many that they are overwhelmed, but enough to make them feel they dressed themselves. Don't try to make them look perfect all the time, like little dolls. And don't make their life one big job interview. If they want to run around the house wearing a bathing suit and a tutu, why not? If they proudly dress themselves in a hilarious combination of stripes and plaids, leggings and shorts — most of it on backwards — congratulate them on their initiative (while encouraging them to tell everyone that *they* did the dressing all by themselves).

As with older children, if they won't wear clothes that are warm enough, let them be cold or wet — again, not enough to get frostbite, but enough to learn the lesson. Just remember that when they're inside, they're warm, and they have trouble imagining that the outside will be different.

19

MESSY ROOM
The Toxic Zone

The Behaviour   It's amazing what can be done with a few apple cores, a week's worth of laundry, and an open box of Lego. Some tiny, minuscule percentage of kids are compulsively neat. The overwhelming majority, however, view the floor of their room as a giant catch basin for everything they own.

Why They Do It   Although the compulsively neat among us can't stand squalor, some people find a certain freedom in a messy room — it can be very exciting. After all, some great work is produced from incredibly cluttered desks. And everyone needs their own space. If you tell your kids what to do with it, it's not really theirs.

Your Reaction   For a lot of parents, the messy room is the bane of their existence. They are afraid their kids will be disorganized when they grow up — that they will become adults who can't find their socks, let alone a job. Others feel it is disrespectful. It offends them just to see it. "Hey!" they think. "The kid is living in a room in *my* house and has to live by *my* standards."

Whatever the reason, knowing there is a festering compost heap upstairs is more than some parents can handle. But fighting over it can be worse than the mess itself.

Your Strategy

Like it or not, it's the kid's room. If you can't handle seeing the mess, make them keep the door shut.

What to Try First

Refuse to go in their room. Tell them it's too messy to even contemplate entering, never mind trying to negotiate a pathway to the bed. They know what this means: no bedtime story and no kiss good night. This is harsh, but effective. And it's not domineering, because you are telling them what *you* will do, not what *they* have to do.

The Practical Stuff

✓ Lead by example. If you are going to make a big deal about their room, you had better be prepared to have yours looking like an army barracks.

✓ If the mess is truly overwhelming, ask if they want some help. If you do help, avoid the clichés that spring unbidden to every parent's lips: "How can you *live* like this?" or "This place looks like a cyclone hit it." If you must comment, at least get someone to write you some new material.

✓ Make sure there are good storage shelves, bins, and containers in your child's room. You can't be too organized when dealing with kids.

✓ Make the bed easy to make — buy duvets that they can just throw over the bed, instead of fussy bedspreads.

✓ Some parents won't let their kids bring friends into their room if it's a mess. This is a mistake. Kids usually value what their peers think. When a friend tells them their room is a pigsty, the message has about ten times more potency than even the most creative of parental reminders.

✓ If all else fails, you can insist that they keep the door closed. This teaches them that what they do affects other people. If you can't stand even *knowing* it's there, admit that this is really your problem.

KEY POINT Look at it this way — losing your favourite jeans in a bottomless heap of clothes, or the hamster in the chaos under the bed, is a great way to experience the consequence of being disorganized. If you keep reminding them to clean up the mess, you take away their responsibility.

Kids Under the Age of Five

Very young kids might feel overwhelmed by the practicalities of cleaning a messy room. In addition to teaching them how to go about cleaning up, you must show them the *value* of a clean room. Make cleaning a part of their daily routine, so that things don't get out of control.

Your underlying attitude should be: "This is your space. If you want me to help you clean it up, I will. If you don't, that's your choice." See #20, on household messiness, for more practical advice.

20

HOUSEHOLD MESSINESS
The Clutter Creators

The Behaviour Some kids travel with a grungy wake of socks, dirty dishes, crumbs, clothes, banana peels, and bits of homework trailing behind them. They create havoc wherever they go. Their room looks like a bomb went off. They cover things in peanut butter, cast their toys to the four winds, track in mud, lose the dog, and can mess up a neat room by just walking through it.

They are, in a word, slobs.

Why They Do It It could be that they are doing it for revenge — they know it drives you nuts and they want to make you angry for whatever reason. It is more likely, however, that you have never taught them how to be organized, or you have nagged them so much they are now "parent deaf."

Your Reaction   Parents who must live with these happy-go-lucky creatures feel used and abused by this lack of respect for the family space. Trying to keep a house presentable is a thankless, nearly impossible task. It is no fun to clean all day, only to see the place in ruins in two minutes. Short of checking into a hotel, there doesn't seem to be a way out of this mess.

Your Strategy   *Get everyone to agree to some hard and fast rules about house maintenance. If they don't stick to the rules, rely on consequences, consequences, and more consequences.*

What to Try First   This is one of those situations where the family meeting saves the day, so make the messy house the first thing on the agenda of your next meeting. Remember, establishing rules and routines is only effective if you can get the kids to agree to them.

Take it problem by problem. Let's say you are annoyed at the crumbs and apple cores in the family room. Instead of finally losing it one day and yelling up the stairwell "That's it! The next person who eats in the family room is dead!" call a meeting and point out the problem. Then ask for suggestions. If nobody has one, calmly suggest a rule that prohibits eating in the family room. If they balk at this, ask them if they would at least be willing to try it out for a week. A rule can always be changed at the next meeting, which makes it easier for them to go along with one they're not crazy about.

Reminders

Once they have agreed to the rules at the family meeting, you have to remind them that they agreed. How you do this is crucial. It's important to get them over the hump and into the routine without turning it into a power struggle.

In the beginning, it's important to be consistent, to remind them every time they forget to put their dish in the sink or hang up their wet bath towel. The real trick is to do it without lecturing or talking too much. Don't "overparent." At the family meeting, encourage everyone to come up with ways they can be reminded. And always try to use the One Word Rule — if they forget to hang up the towel, just say "towel." This keeps the aggravation factor to a minimum.

The Practical Stuff

Help them to be organized. Sometimes kids have so much stuff that it overwhelms them. You can help by periodically rotating some of their toys in and out of storage. Next, go through each room in the house and see what is out of place. Then make sure there is a place for each item, and that the child can easily use it. For example, if the washcloth is lying in the tub, provide a hook for it. Here are some other examples:

✓ Put up special hooks (at their height) so they can hang up their jackets.

✓ Have different boxes and shelves for different sizes of toys: one for dolls, one for big stuff, one for dress-up clothes, etc.

✓ Hang the clothes rack in their closet at a height they can actually use.

✓ For younger kids, use bins instead of a dresser to make it easier for them to put clothes away themselves. Label them with pictures of the clothes that go there.

KEY POINT It's important to include the kids in the solution and not simply impose it upon them. Get it through your head that kids are your partners — and treat them as such. Keep the discussions friendly. All this greatly increases the chance that they will go along with it.

Consequences

Backing up all the agreements and reminders are the logical consequences that result when the new rules are broken. The consequences should also be endorsed by everyone at the family meeting; otherwise, the kids will feel resentful and stubborn. Bring it up after a particularly messy day: "Nobody put their dishes away after dinner. What should we do about it?"

The consequences should be logical — they must make sense in order to differentiate them from punishment. For example:

• If they leave their toys out, collect them in a big box that you keep in the furnace room. Retrieving the toys becomes a pain in the neck (and the bigger the box, the greater the inconvenience). If their messiness persists, they can't have the confiscated toys back until they feel they can pick up after themselves.

- If they don't put their bikes away at night, they might get stolen. Don't let them ride their bikes until they learn to be more responsible.
- If they won't clean up their room, they have to keep their door closed. And because you are disgusted by the mess, you won't be able to go in to read them a bedtime story or put away their laundry. See **#19** for advice on dealing with a messy room.

FACING FEARS AND ANXIETIES

21

IRRATIONAL FEARS
The Monster Under the Bed

The Behaviour   Yes, there is a monster who lives under every kid's bed. Adults don't believe it, but kids know it's true. A hyperactive imagination can prevent a normal, well-adjusted kid from falling asleep at night, or wake her up in a sweat at 4 a.m. During the day, it can make her reluctant to let go of your pantleg, or run screaming at the sight of good old uncle Oscar.

Why They Do It   Irrational fears are the price of an imagination so vivid, it can turn a shadow on the wall into something horrific enough to curdle Dracula's blood. Another problem is that kids are such tiny people, with such limited knowledge of the world, that to them, anything they imagine *could* be true. A barking dog could be merely a noisy animal, or a hungry kid-eater with a taste for three-year-olds.

A stranger could be a saint, or someone who just rose from the grave. How's a kid to know? Of course, fear is not always bad — after all, a healthy fear of being run over by a garbage truck teaches kids to be cautious. But many childhood fears are irrational. In fact, your child can become so terrified, it's scary.

Your Reaction

Depending on the circumstances, either annoyance or heart-rending concern.

Your Strategy

The less fuss you make about it, the quicker it will go away. But understand that no matter what you think, the fear is real to them. Above all, radiate calm so they learn that the object of their fear really isn't dangerous.

What to Try First

The most important thing to remember when your child is freaking out about something is that you mustn't overreact. Be matter-of-fact. Reassure them. Don't belittle them by telling them to "stop acting like a baby." They aren't. They're acting like kids, which is what they are. For them, the *Creature from the Black Lagoon* actually exists.

Next, engage the child in finding a solution, by saying something like: "Life is full of little problems and this is just one of them. Let's figure out how to solve it." Now she's not in it alone. Get her to come up with some suggestions, and use them if they are even remotely realistic. You can nudge her in the right direction: "If you think there is a monster in the closet, is there anything you can do with the door to make it less scary? Keep the door open so you can see what's inside it? That's a good idea."

By coming up with their own ideas, kids learn that there is always a solution, and that they have at least some control over their lives and their fears.

The Practical Stuff

✓ If the child wants a night light, give her one, or suggest it yourself. Let her know you are nearby in case a tentacle comes snaking over the bed. But watch out — if she thinks she can get attention with her fear, she'll have you running in to help every five minutes.

✓ If the child wants to avoid a fearful situation — like crossing the road to keep away from a dog that always barks at him — let him do it. Of course, you could also encourage him to walk past the dog accompanied by friends, or have a dog of his own to protect him. The only caveat is that you shouldn't let the child's fear control the family, or force you to walk ten miles out of your way.

KEY POINT Most childhood fears are normal and temporary. They can be very intense for the short time they are around, but usually they dissipate quickly. On the other hand, if the fears are starting to rule your kid's life, you might wish to seek professional help.

Do's

✓ Do be careful about what they watch on TV. Young kids can't handle scary movies. You don't have to protect them from every questionable image; just use your head and screen what they see. Watch movies with them. Explain how the special effects are done, and teach them that it's not real. Ask them to imagine the lights and the director off-camera — they'll realize that *TV* is fantasy, and *life* is reality.

✓ Do be discreet when discussing the news with your spouse over breakfast. Kids pick up more than you think. Idle talk about the latest mass murderer or other weird crime may react with their fertile imaginations to produce obsessive fears.

Don'ts

✗ Don't overemphasize the sinister aspect of strangers when street-proofing your kids.

✗ Don't push him into situations he fears. Trying to desensitize kids can backfire. It's okay to expose him to a cute puppy to get him over a fear of big dogs, but if he doesn't want to look at snakes, he shouldn't have to.

22

FEAR OF FAILURE
The Little Engine That Couldn't

The Behaviour It's one thing to have a kid who likes to pull dangerous stunts like jumping from one roof to another. It's
quite another to have a kid who won't go down a
four-foot slide. Some kids won't try anything. They
will stand on the side of the pool for hours, afraid to
jump in. Or they'll reject a new game because they
are afraid to lose. Everything — from learning to
write to riding a two-wheeler — is fraught with danger or the distinct possibility of failure. They give up
the first time something goes wrong — and something *always* goes wrong. When that happens, they
usually blame themselves. They don't have much fun
and they're not much fun to be around.

Why They Do It Quite simply, these kids compare themselves to
others and feel inadequate. They want to be left

alone, believing that "no risk" equals "no failure." They have also learned that if you "can't" do something, then someone else has to do it for you.

In some cases, children won't try because they can't stand second-place. They are very hard on themselves and extremely concerned about what others think of them. The super-perfectionist has to get it right the first time, not realizing that skills are mastered over time.

Your Reaction

Knowing that your child feels like an inadequate kid makes you feel like an inadequate parent. And when they won't even try something you know they could do, you feel disappointed. You can't stand to see your child moping on the beach while the other kids frolic in the surf. How can you get them into the swim of life?

Your Strategy

Be patient. Make a big deal about any effort they make on their own. Give them the courage to be imperfect.

What to Try First

Build up his confidence by providing a lot of training before asking him to jump in and try. When it comes to sports, roll the ball at first instead of throwing it. Be very encouraging, even if he just *tries* to catch it. Start with activities that won't be too hard. For example, swimming is easier for most kids than baseball. Team sports where no one can be singled out for losing — like tug of war — are also good bets. Raise their expectations little by little.

The Practical Stuff

✓ Base your comments on the effort she is making, not the quality of the results. If she starts to write, mention what "a beautiful letter B that is," while ignoring the unintelligible letter S. If you correct her too much, she will see it as proof that she is incompetent.

KEY POINT Even though they like to drop out of things, try to keep them involved. They need a great deal of encouragement to keep at it.

Do's

✓ Do encourage your child to try even when they fail. Emphasize the enjoyment of the process, rather than the outcome, with hopeful comments such as:

- "Don't give up."
- "Even though you don't think you can do it, I know you can and I'm not going to give up on you."
- "You've really improved. Last week you couldn't do this. Now you can."
- And the old standby — "Nice try."

✓ Do help them lower their standards by reminding them (with a friendly tone of acceptance) that "Nobody's perfect" or "Everyone makes mistakes."

Don'ts

✗ Don't rush them into things. Some four-year-olds really are too young for piano lessons. Even playing "Chopsticks" can be overwhelming.

✗ Don't compare them to other kids. Don't make such a big deal about where they rank in school. For a perfectionist, even being number two can be a disaster.

✗ Don't be critical. This is a good rule for all kids, but especially for kids who won't try. Give them a break by avoiding remarks like:

- "You're not trying hard enough."
- "You could do better."
- "Your three-year-old sister could do it better than that."

23

SHYNESS
The Power of Passivity

The Behaviour   Some of us have painful memories of being socially awkward when we were young. That's why it breaks our hearts to see our youngster all alone, staring at the floor, while someone's birthday party goes on merrily around her. Shy kids have trouble making friends. Because life is endlessly social, kids who are unable to "play the game" make everyone uncomfortable. And when you introduce your shy kid to strangers, everyone stares down at her as she hides behind your legs.

"She's just a little shy," you say apologetically.

They smile and nod, but inside you know they're thinking, "Here's a kid that's going to stay home with a good book on prom night."

Why They Do It   Shy kids often compare themselves to others and are scared to death of making a mistake (sound familiar?). Their shyness can be intensified if they have a social whiz for a sibling, with whom they feel they can't compete. Recent research indicates that some shyness may even be genetic.

Your Reaction

You try to turn them on socially, but everything you do just drives them deeper into their shell. How can you turn your wallflower into an effervescent rose?

Your Strategy

It's up to your child whether or not to get involved socially. But you can help by building up their self-confidence, and encouraging them to be more assertive.

What to Try First

When the old hide-behind-mom-and-dad's-legs routine starts, ignore it. Don't coax or try to physically bring the kid out. Let them move at their own speed. Introduce them in a normal way and if they don't respond, change the subject. If the other person says something like "Oh, he's shy, eh?" respond with "No, he's not shy. He'll talk to you when he's ready."

You do this for two reasons. One is that if you keep telling the kid he's shy you give him a discouraging label, which tends to reinforce the shyness. The other is that some kids are naturally not as outgoing as others and, to a degree, that's all right.

The Practical Stuff

Interestingly enough, shyness can be a clever way to attract undue attention. When you are shy you stand out just as you do when you are loud and aggressive. In other words, it's hard to ignore someone who is ignoring you. Although this goal is unconscious in your shy kid, if you make a show of trying to draw them out they can dig in their heels, protesting: "You can't make me respond!" And they may come to enjoy the spotlight their shyness throws on them.

Do's

✓ Do give them tips on how to be social. Role play to help her learn how to "break the ice" with other kids. Pretending you don't know your child, walk up to her and ask: "Do you want to play? We could take turns pushing each other on the swing."

✓ Do show them how to break into a strange group if they want to play. Usually all they need do is walk over and slowly integrate themselves, at their own speed, into the play. But you have to make your child *believe* this will work.

✓ Do build them up by commenting on their strengths. Shy kids lack the courage to face rejection. If they have a great sense of humour or are good at sports, tell them. Point out (if you think it's true) that "Tommy really likes you." Shy kids are usually very sensitive.

✓ Do let your kids learn from you. They are very observant — let them see you interacting socially.

Don'ts

✗ Don't keep pushing them to "say hello to uncle Jim." It's embarrassing — and a turnoff — to be asked to perform. Besides, a five-year-old knows how to say hello without being told. They will come around when they get older.

✗ Don't let them withdraw. Make sure they learn social skills by spending time in groups: enrol them in day care, Brownies or Cubs, and play groups. The more practice they get, the better their social skills will become. CAUTION: Don't push the social stuff too much. These kids enjoy and need time to themselves.

✗ Don't push them to be friends with everyone. Often for a shy kid, one very close friend is enough.

LEARNING TO TAKE RESPONSIBILITY

24

FORGETFULNESS
"Has Anyone Seen My Head?"

The Behaviour   If you find yourself telling your child that she would forget her head if it wasn't screwed on, you have this problem. She forgets her lunch, so you have to bring it to her. She forgets her gloves somewhere and you have to buy new ones. She forgets her homework and you look like a bad parent.

Why They Do It   Forgetfulness is a sign of irresponsibility — after all, they can probably remember parties, or when their favourite TV show is on. If your kids forget, it's probably because you are doing their remembering for them. Also, kids are not that future-oriented. They are so involved in the present that they can't imagine being cold or hungry two hours from now.

Your Reaction	You spend half your time following them around with reminders like: "Don't forget your hat! Don't forget your knapsack!" It's so bad you forget what it's like *not* to remind them.
Your Strategy	*Make remembering things their responsibility. Accomplish this by creating routines and allowing them to experience consequences.*
What to Try First	The best way to teach your kid how to remember is to create routines (like the ones that make *your* life bearable), so they can rely on good habits rather than a good memory.

The Practical Stuff

✓ Have a meeting with your kids and suggest that because they are forgetting so many important things, the whole family should try to come up with ways to help them remember. Let everyone brainstorm creative ways to remember to feed the cat or take out the garbage. Pick the best ideas.

✓ Post a checklist of things that have to be done at critical times: before bed; before school; preparing for the next day; and so on. Then, let the kids follow through without you hovering over the list.

✓ Ask, don't tell. For example, when they are getting dressed for school, ask them: "What else do you need?" When they say "I need gloves," nod your head in agreement. This prods the kid to think, and it avoids power struggles. If he starts to walk out without a hat, let him know it's freezing out, but let him make the decision. If they forget to put the milk away, casually drop a remark like: "Is there anything you forgot to do?" Or, remind them indirectly by saying out loud what *you* have to remember: "It's raining today, I'd better bring my umbrella and wear my boots."

✓ By all means, teach them to remember, but don't be so quick to remind them if they forget. Let them experience the inconveniences of forgetfulness. If they forget their lunch, they go hungry. If they forget their gym clothes, they have to sit on the sidelines. If they don't wear their rainboots, they have wet feet for a day. If they don't put the portable phone back where it belongs, they can't use it until they can remember to do it. By the age of seven or eight kids should be able to take care of most aspects of their lives, but some parents won't let them.

KEY POINT Don't pamper. Pampering parents don't want their kids to ever be uncomfortable. The result is that pampering parents have forgetful children who don't *have* to remember anything.

25

MISHANDLING MONEY
A Tiny Little Fistful of Dollars

The Behaviour To kids, money is like magic — it just seems to appear. They don't understand where it comes from or the concept of saving it. Anyone who has seen their child blow a week's allowance on teeth-rotting jujubes in twenty seconds flat is all too aware of this phenomenon.

Why They Do It They mishandle money because they don't know any better. You want your kids to know that money has real worth — that it's not just something the Bank of Mom and Dad doles out periodically. But why should they save when they know that eventually you will buy them whatever it is they want? If you say you can't afford to buy something, they think you are being mean: "Use your credit card, Mom."

Your Reaction

You're usually too busy trying to balance your out-of-whack budget to notice their lack of monetary savvy, but you do have concerns. Is it okay to pay them to do chores? What if they won't help at all unless you pay them? They can't even legally baby-sit until they are twelve years old. How are they going to learn about one of the most important aspects of the adult world?

Your Strategy

Give them an allowance that is broken down into money for treats and money for items that don't benefit them directly, such as gifts or savings.

What to Try First

Giving kids their own lump of money on a regular basis is the opposite of pampering, which consists of giving them everything they want whenever they ask for it. You should begin with an allowance as soon as they start to ask for things in stores (at age three or four). You can teach them about saving when they are seven or eight. Don't try before, because kids younger than that live in the present, with little appreciation for the future.

The Practical Stuff

✓ The allowance could be broken down something like this: Out of a total of four dollars, fifty cents could be for gifts, one dollar could go in the bank, and the rest is their mad money.

✓ Their mad money portion can be based on what you would normally buy them as a treat every week — a candy bar for a young child, or a trip to the movies and a comic book for an older one. From then on, the treats are up to them. If they blow it all, they learn the lesson that anyone who has taken a pair of scissors to their credit card knows: Once your money is gone, you have to do without.

✓ If they want something big and expensive, don't trip over yourself to buy it for them. Let them save for it. This teaches them how to make choices — a handful of jujubes now, or a life-size chocolate bunny next month. The main point here is that you are teaching them how to budget money. Let them make mistakes. Advise them: "I don't think that's a well-made toy." If it breaks, don't say "I told you so." Let them learn it themselves.

✓ Encourage them to save in order to buy gifts for others. This will teach them the joy of giving.

✓ When they are around twelve or thirteen, you can give them a clothes budget. Figure out what you would normally spend for their clothes and give it to them, perhaps in seasonal payments.

Do's

✓ Do use their allowance to make restitution. Say they break someone's toy in anger or smash a door on purpose. Why should others suffer? Send your kid the bill. If they won't brush their teeth and the dentist bill is higher, make them pay a part of it.

✓ Do open a bank account for them.

✓ Do decide what you will buy before you go shopping, and let the kids know it. You don't want them to see you doing a lot of impulse buying. If you went for groceries, don't let them talk you into barrettes and toy necklaces.

✓ Do teach them the value of money: "With your four dollars you could buy this jewellery box (which will last), or a crate of licorice pipes (which won't)."

Don'ts

✗ Don't use the allowance to manipulate their behaviour. Money will push them around enough later in life.

✗ Don't lecture them (or even point it out) if they make a stupid purchase, or trade a Barbie doll for a dead frog. Trust them to figure it out themselves.

Hiring the Vertically Challenged

Encouraging your kids to make their own money, when they are old enough to have a paper route or cut lawns, is a great idea. Hiring them to do chores around the house is not. They should help out for the greater benefit of the family, not for personal gain. Start doing this and they won't wash the car or do the dishes without a retainer. Does anyone pay you to tuck them in or do their laundry?

26

SHIRKING HOUSEHOLD CHORES
"Your Job Is to Work. My Job Is to Have Fun."

The Behaviour   The subtitle just about sums it up. You spend your time cleaning and cooking and making countless grilled cheese sandwiches, and your kids spend their time having a ball. Requests for help are met with pained expressions and lame excuses. Either they're in the middle of their favourite TV show, or it's not *their* job, or — when they're at their most esoteric — it's just not fair.

Why They Do It   Often they are used to having things done for them by pampering parents. And these days, many two-income families hire cleaning help to do things for the parents *and* the kids. But the short answer is, if your kids won't help it's because they haven't been encouraged to.

Your Reaction You alternate between feeling like a slave and acting like a prison guard. Why can't your kids see that work around the house should be done by everyone? How can you get them to take responsibility for doing their share?

Your Strategy *Even if it's easier for you to do things yourself, get the kids to help very early in life (at the beginning of their second year). For older kids, use logical consequences.*

What to Try First Your kids have to realize that helping out is a privilege, not a chore. For the best way to present this, read the scene in *Tom Sawyer* about whitewashing the fence. Believe it or not, kids really do like to help — they want to feel useful and significant. As parents you should harness this most wonderful attribute, and make it work for you before chores become an issue in a power struggle. Start as soon as they show an interest in helping. If you don't believe they really *can* help, go to a farm sometime and see what very young kids are capable of doing. TIP: With young boys, it's good if Dad also helps so they don't get the idea that helping is something only girls do.

The Practical Stuff ✓ Do chores together. You may wish to have a Saturday morning chore time. Make it fun. While you're working, put on some music that everyone loves. Order a pizza or rent a video after the work is over. Teach them that work is fulfilling, not a punishment. This kind of thing keeps the family close.

✓ Let younger kids follow you around and imitate what you do: dusting, raking leaves, shovelling the sidewalk, baking cookies. Here are some jobs even a four-year-old can do:

- sweeping
- sorting the laundry
- setting the table
- putting groceries away in low cupboards
- feeding the fish
- bringing in the morning paper
- watering the plants
- dusting
- vacuuming (They love it. In fact, we wish someone would market a vacuum cleaner designed especially for little kids.)

✓ If a toddler wants to wash the kitchen floor with you, mark off a part of the floor for them. Give them a small watering can for the plants.

✓ Older kids can do almost everything else, from clearing the table and washing the dishes, to yard work and washing the car.

KEY POINT A lot of these jobs are more easily and efficiently done by someone older, but it's worth putting up with some less than perfect work. Teaching your kids now will pay big dividends later. Besides, watching a two-year-old trying to sweep is so cute it hurts.

Do's

✓ Do have a family meeting and draw up a list of what has to be done. Decide how the jobs will be assigned: either they can choose them, or the jobs can be rotated.

✓ Do put a job chart on the fridge or bulletin board. Let them change it themselves so they don't feel trapped.

✓ Do overlook imperfect work. They'll get discouraged if you criticize their efforts.

Don'ts

✗ Don't pay them for the jobs. It's great to give them an allowance before they are able to earn their own money (see **#25** on money matters), but as we have said, housework is not an odious chore they have to be compensated for. Teach them that work has to be shared by everyone in the family, along with the goodies you all enjoy.

✗ Don't demand that they drop what they are doing and help in the middle of their favourite show or project. Try to set chore-times that everyone agrees to — this avoids conflict. And if you have to ask for something that's not on the list, ask politely, the way you would ask an adult.

✗ Don't nag or constantly remind them if they miss their chores. Let them experience the consequences (see below). If they don't do the dishes as agreed, they don't have anything clean to eat from at the next meal. Stifle the urge to do it yourself. Let them eat their beef stew over the kitchen sink. Or maybe the consequence is that dinner can't be served. Of course you too have to put up with the inconvenience, but is the alternative — endless nagging — really any better? It's in your long-term interest to teach them once and for all.

✗ Don't moan and whine about your own jobs — as always, you're the model.

Consequences

Here are some examples of logical consequences for shirking chores. Let your imagination run wild and come up with your own. Just make sure the consequence has a clear connection to the uncooperative behaviour.

- Grass is not cut. CONSEQUENCE: The yard is off-limits. Can't have friends over to play in the yard.
- Won't take out the garbage. CONSEQUENCE: Put the stinky bag in their room.
- Food is left out on the counter. CONSEQUENCE: Can't have supper because there is no room to prepare it.

HELPFUL HINT Some things don't have a logical

consequence. The best way to deal with this situation is to bring it up at the next meeting: "You said you would fold the laundry and didn't?" Then ask (with curiosity, not anger): "What happened?" From there you can explore what can be done about it. Rather than attacking the child's character, you try to solve the problem.

The Ultimate Consequence

In an *extreme* situation, where the kids have dug in their heels and refused to do anything, there is one truly awesome consequence — the general strike! You say: "So, you don't want to do any work around the house. I'll tell you what — let's *all* try that. None of us will do any work and see what it's like. Does that sound fair?"

Life now becomes very surreal, because this means no grocery shopping gets done, no cleaning, no driving them anywhere, no laundry, no meals are cooked — nothing. This is, of course, madness, but we know from personal experience that an emergency family meeting will be called within three days. If nothing else, this is a great way to teach kids exactly what adults do for them. CAUTION: This has to be done in the right spirit.

FIVE
MINUTES FOR
FIGHTING

27

BULLYING
"Hey Twinkie, Gimme a Quarter!"

The Behaviour The bully has cast his malevolent shadow over many a recess. This is the kind of kid who enjoys intimidating others, especially if they are smaller. The cartoon image of the bully is the big lumbering male kid with the brushcut and the nickname "Spike," but these days girls are starting to fill the role as well. The bully is often violent, and will extort money and break up friendly games for the fun of it. And who's the easiest target for the discriminating bully? Her younger siblings.

Why They Do It Kids like this often feel overpowered and pushed around themselves. To overcompensate, they learn how to be powerful by watching others, especially their parents. If you are a "power parent," always screaming and ordering your family around, you are the perfect role model for the bully.

Your Reaction

Usually it's to bully them right back, but some parents are actually intimidated by their bullying offspring, who threaten to smash up the house and may even resort to smacking old Mom and Pop around.

Your Strategy

Be firm without domineering. Give them jobs with power they can use to help people.

What to Try First

This kind of kid already feels like an outcast. Your job is to make him feel like a part of something — the family or the community. By always taking sides against him, you reinforce his tendency to see himself as an outlaw.

KEY POINT Don't follow your natural impulse to bully him back. It not only starts a vicious circle, it

may even be how he got this way in the first place. To change your kid you might have to change the way *you* operate. Stop bossing people around. Instead, tell your kids what you will do. Rather than commanding them to "make your lunch *now* or you're going to be sorry!" say something like: "I'll put out your lunch fixings, but you are responsible for making it." If they don't make it, they are hungry. This approach not only works better, it minimizes the possibility of behaviour aimed at getting power or revenge.

The Practical Stuff

It's most important to teach this kid to have compassion for other people. Here's how:

- ✓ Give them the power — if you know they won't abuse it — to do good. Make them the crossing guard, the baby sitter, the hall monitor, or a team leader or referee.

- ✓ Share the power of the family with them. Ask for their opinions and ideas: Where should we put the swings? How can I fix this door? What should we do Friday night? Get them to order the pizza, book tickets, or co-pilot with the map on long drives.

- ✓ Talk about how other people feel when bad things happen — not as a lecture but simply in conversation. Use books and movies as starting points to discussions about concepts like fairness, ethics, other people's feelings, etc. Ask him things like: "How do you think someone would feel if they were pushed off the swings?" Don't direct the example at him or he will feel blamed and turn off. Talk about the situation as if it is a story you have heard.

- ✓ Get agreement (at a family meeting) to some good rules that raise your family's moral tone.

Establish rules like: no racist or sexist jokes; no embarrassing people in public; no hurting, shouting, or stealing.

✓ Be loving and affectionate, no matter what. Let them know that even when they do hurtful things, you still love them. Convince them you believe they can change. When you notice improvement, comment on it. Be patient. This problem will take time.

Consequences

✓ Obviously, they can't play with other kids, or perhaps even go to school, until they have learned not to throw their weight around. Staying in, playing alone, or even suspension from school might be in order.

✓ If they break or take things, they must compensate the owner with their own money.

HELPFUL HINT Violent kids can become dangerous, especially to younger siblings. If things start to get out of control, get outside help in the form of family counselling.

28

FIGHTING WITH FRIENDS
"Are You Talkin' to Me?"

The Behaviour

One of the most amazing things about young children is how they will stop playing with a dollhouse or a video game if one of their friends is playing with a piece of wood. Suddenly, because their friend has it, that crummy piece of wood is the greatest toy in the world. A fight breaks out and parents rush from every direction to break it up. This can go on all day, as kids who are actually good friends alternate between sweet playtime and sudden flare-ups.

Why They Do It

When kids fight with their friends, they are defining their relationships — who will be the boss, or the follower, or the idea person, and so on. With toddlers, it's simply because they lack the skills to solve problems in any other way.

Your Reaction   Invariably, your first reaction is to break up a fight between kids. As a result, you spend half your time being a referee. Why can't kids quietly harbour resentments, like adults?

Your Strategy   *Unless you think someone is going to get really hurt, let them work it out. Never take sides.*

What to Try First   Ignore them. Interfering, although it deals with the immediate problem, doesn't teach kids problem-solving skills. It can also create resentments if you take sides. Besides, they usually resolve it fairly quickly, because it's more fun to play than to fight.

The Practical Stuff

✓ Some kids run to Mom and Dad over every little dispute. This is tattling. Whatever you do, don't encourage it. Other kids don't like tattlers getting them into trouble. At the very least, it harms their relationships. Discourage tattling by encouraging them to solve their own problems. At the same time, let them know they can turn to you in a crisis.

✓ Kids are more possessive on their own turf. Younger children in particular have trouble sharing their toys. Take them to a neutral corner, such as a park or playground, where nobody has any toys to protect.

✓ Fighting is common, but that doesn't mean it should be excused. To help prevent it, teach your kids the value of sharing. Play games with them. Say things like "Can I play with that when you're done?" to give them an idea of how people can share. If there is a problem, help them work it out non-violently. Make sure they follow the rules of a game, because that teaches them orderliness and how to lose gracefully.

HELPFUL HINT You can distract toddlers from fighting by offering them an alternative: if they are fighting over a rubber duck, entice one of them with a jack-in-the-box. This takes advantage of their short attention span.

Do's

✓ Do teach them hospitality. Tell them the guest is special and should go first.

✓ Do make a point of noticing when they do resolve differences or share things with friends. We are usually quick to point out when a kid screws up. See how fast you can be when they do something right.

✓ Do make sure your kids see you sharing things. Make a big deal of sharing a piece of your chocolate cake with someone, no matter how close to impossible this may be for you.

✓ Do consult with your kid. If you know she has trouble with a particular friend, ask her beforehand how she thinks she could prevent a fight.

✓ Do teach kids to compromise. If they both insist on playing with the same dump truck, have them use an egg timer and switch when the sand runs out. This only works if they both agree to it.

✓ Do avoid social situations when your kids are tired and you know they'll have a short fuse. If you *have* to go somewhere, get ready to leave when you see them starting to fall apart. Don't wait until your child is homicidal.

✓ Do let your kid spend some time alone if he is fighting a lot. Let him decide when to get back in the social whirl by saying: "You let me know when you're ready to see your friends again."

Don'ts

✗ Don't force two kids to play together if they really don't hit it off.

✗ Don't instill competition in your kids. Buy and play cooperative games. You can even change some popular games. For example: Play musical chairs, only have the odd person out sit on someone's knee, rather than leave the game. This encourages kids to solve the problem of the missing chair. Stress fun over winning.

29

FIGHTING WITH SIBLINGS
Living with the Enemy

The Behaviour In most houses, brothers and sisters fight with each other. It doesn't have to be this way, but it is. Verbal fencing and even knock-down-drag-'em-out fights can happen at any time. It's like living in a war zone. They will fight over anything: toys, TV shows, or a piece of dirt — it doesn't matter. They will also fight at the most inconvenient times: in the back of the car at rush hour, when you're out for dinner, or in front of the boss. Occasionally (but less than you might think) they will even hurt each other.

Why They Do It When two kids fight, they have agreed to misbehave in order to get attention. Sometimes they do it because they really don't like each other, but that is rare. Kids compete for your attention in ways that you would never imagine. Pay close attention and you will find that one always plays the good child and one the bad. It may not be brilliant but it works.

Then there are the resentments felt by the older child when the new baby comes home from the hospital, pushing her off the throne. "Why don't you take him back now, Mom, or trade him in for a puppy," she asks, while giving a few sly pinches to this usurper of parental attention.

Your Reaction

You want a harmonious house, but it's hard to achieve. No matter what the cause, when siblings turn their energy against each other, it's a jungle out there.

Your Strategy

You may not realize it, but your kids almost always fight to get your attention. So unless you think someone is going to end up in the hospital, stay out of it.

What to Try First

Your job is to create a non-competitive family so your kids can find their roles in non-competitive ways. Decreasing competition also improves their relationships with each other. The best way to do this is to refuse to take sides. Don't always go running as soon as the gloves come off, asking what happened and then acting as judge and jury. Let the kids learn how to work it out for themselves. If you interfere, *you* are supplying the solution, which teaches them nothing. Sometimes they will come up with a solution you wouldn't have picked — for instance, instead of sharing a toy, they might each decide to play with something else — but it works for them.

HELPFUL HINT Of course, if you think one of the participants is really going to get hurt, send them to neutral corners (like their rooms).

The Practical Stuff

When the new baby shows up:

✓ Watch how you treat the older kids. It's natural to try and protect the baby: "Shhhhh. The baby is sleeping. Go away and be quiet!" This is guaranteed to create a feeling of resentment.

✓ Give positive attention to older kids by accentuating what is going right: "You're very good with the baby." "You're a big help." "Gee, the baby is just crazy about you."

✓ Plan lots of quality, one-on-one time with the older kids.

✓ Make the other child feel important by helping you with the baby. Don't make it your baby, make it *our* baby. Let the older one read a book with you while you're nursing. Any child can pour baby food out of the jar or bring a diaper. An older child can even diaper the baby, relieving you of your favourite job.

Do's

✓ Do encourage siblings to help each other. Kids are great teachers and this role will greatly change the relationship between them.

✓ Do try to play non-competitive games as a family. If everyone enjoys skating, for example, do it more often.

✓ Do bring up any legitimate beefs the kids may have about each other (after the dust has settled), and include everyone in finding ways to solve them. It's not good to go to bed angry, so try to resolve them before everyone goes to bed. Work on rules that prevent fighting: "Is the computer in Jenny's room for her or for the whole family?"

✓ Do use the ancient practice of banishment. Send them outside if they insist on fighting. Since the main reason they are fighting is usually to get your attention, this is no fun for them. You'd be surprised how often two kids going at it like a couple of wolverines will suddenly lose interest once the audience is gone. You have also treated them as a group instead of assigning blame. This not only keeps the house harmonious, it prevents the creation of a punishment "food chain," in which the bigger kid gets punished and punches out a younger kid, who then takes it out on anyone smaller than him until the youngest smacks her teddy bear. It also teaches them about the rights of others.

✓ Do be a good role model. Make sure they don't see *you* arguing in a disrespectful way (yelling, name calling, throwing dinner plates). Cooperate with your spouse because kids will model after a power parent and start to believe that fighting is okay. When you do have problems, let them see you working it out peacefully.

✓ Do try and tune out the fighting, even if you have to leave the scene. You need the patience of Job for this one, but remember, if you stop the attention, you stop a lot of the fighting.

✓ Do use the family meeting for problems the kids can't work out themselves. Use reflective listening (see #5 for tips) and brainstorming (a technique where everyone tries to come up with solutions to a problem). Let them know they can agree to disagree. Try saying: "I know you two really *do* like each other. I'm sure you can work it out." Comment on it when they do work well together.

✓ Do allow kids to talk about their siblings (at a neutral time), even if their feelings are negative.

Don'ts

✗ Don't compartmentalize your kids by labelling them: "She's the academic one." "He's so social." "She's musical."

✗ Don't have favourites. If one child feels that another gets more love, or attention, or special treatment, they resent it and may even think they have nothing to lose. And don't compare them: "Why can't you pick up after yourself like your sister?" That one is just guaranteed to send them looking — eyes narrowed and fists balled — for their obsessively neat sister.

✗ Don't fall for the one who always plays the "victim" to get your sympathy. Instead, teach them how to stand up for themselves.

30

ARGUING WITH PARENTS
"Your Honour, I Object!"

The Behaviour

If you love to debate, you'll love having kids with this misbehaviour. If not, it's like living with a little F. Lee Bailey on a big fat retainer. You say it's time for bed and they plead and argue: "It's not fair. Please let me stay up." As they grow older, they'll begin to argue over *really* important things, such as: "Please let me have a ring in my nose. It's not fair, all the other kids have them."

Some kids just have to take a contrary position. They will argue about absolutely anything. However, we're not talking about intellectual, Socratic arguments over abstract principles. When kids argue with their parents, it's a struggle over pure power, in which the combatants slug it out over the minutiae of family life.

Why They Do It

Arguing is about winning. It's about outsmarting you. From the kid's point of view, defeating you with logic and reasoning is a victory to be savoured. Or it may be enough just to watch the parent lose control while they remain calm. Think about it: you throw down your paper and stomp off sputtering with rage, while they stand calm and composed with a quizzical look. Who do you think won that one?

Your Reaction

Even though you think you are smarter than them, you can't win because it's their game. Only they know the rules, which means they have a lot more patience than you have. Despite your best intentions, you end up stalking off in a huff, your dignity in tatters, wondering why they argue so much and how you can win once in a while.

Your Strategy

Argue less. Listen more. It takes two to argue, and if you don't join in, there's no payoff for your kid.

What to Try First

If a contentious issue comes up, take your stand, say your peace, and let them say theirs.

Be flexible. Keep the carved-in-stone rules — no playing in the street, no lighting matches under the Christmas tree — to a minimum. If you are too rigid, your kids will follow suit.

The Practical Stuff

Once all the facts have been trotted out and everyone has had their say, either come to an agreement or agree to disagree. One way to agree with an argumentative kid is to brainstorm. Make a list of all the points to consider, pro and con. Draw a line through the ideas nobody likes. From what's left, agree on something that you *both* can live with.

These kinds of kids can't stand being told what to do. They desperately need a say in what happens in their lives. Give it to them. You have to give up a little control, which is scary, but in the long run your kid will be less argumentative and more independent. As parenting expert Barbara Coloroso puts it, you can afford to compromise on things that are not "unethical, immoral, or dangerous."

KEY POINT Make sure you really *listen* to them, and that they *hear* you listening (see **#5** for listening tips). Demand that they hear you out, but — and this is very important — make sure you give them credit for their point of view. Say things like "I never thought of that before" or "Now that's an interesting point of view." Resist the temptation to say this sarcastically.

Do's

✓ Do use family meetings to hammer out rules or changes to rules. If they start arguing to stay up an extra hour on Friday night because one of their favourite shows is on later, take it up at the next meeting. This prevents arguments from erupting, and keeps the discussion within the civilized structure of the meeting. Keep the agenda posted on a chart. Add to it when there is a problem by saying: "I see this is a problem. I'll write it down and we'll talk about it at the meeting on Saturday."

✓ Do take a look at your marriage. Are you giving your kids the idea that arguing is how you are *supposed* to solve problems?

Don'ts

✗ Whatever you do, don't let arguments go on and on. If they won't stop, either leave the room or ask them to leave. Make an "I" statement like: "I don't want to argue now." Walking away from an argument doesn't mean the kid won. It means you have chosen not to argue. But be consistent. If you cave in to arguments, count on having your house turned into a courtroom until your kid starts her own practice.

✗ Don't give them secret encouragement. Sometimes the parents of argumentative kids are domineering, righteous, and manipulative themselves. Arguing is how the kid has learned to get the upper hand. That sometimes makes these same parents secretly proud of their contentious offspring. The message is: "Stop doing this but, doggone it, you sure are a chip off the old block."

The Up Side of Kids Who Argue

Argumentative kids are assertive, clever, and involved, and they make excellent leaders. They are always thinking of ways to make their life better.

Arguers tend to be both optimistic and tenacious. They are acutely concerned with the notion of justice, of what is and is not fair. And yes, they probably would make good lawyers.

HITTING THE BOOKS

31

CLASSROOM MISBEHAVIOUR
Send in the Class Clowns

The Behaviour   Some kids seem to like spending their days depriving their classmates of an education. This can manifest in lots of ways: fighting, giggling, fooling around, not listening, and talking back. With thirty or forty kids in one room, there are necessarily a lot of rules, and a lot of chances to break them. Who can resist making a funny face when thirty kids break up? And the old turning-the-eyelids-inside-out trick is a guaranteed blockbuster. They pass notes, figure out the correct spelling of obscene words on the blackboard, and accurately hurl spitballs into each other's eyes. Anything to keep from learning. If all else fails, smart-mouthing the teacher is a sure way to create a *Rebel Without a Cause* image.

Why They Do It   We all find social significance in our roles: mother, father, bread-winner, weekend barbecue chef, etc. The child who is running amok in the classroom is getting her significance from her role as the rebel or the class clown. The reason is as old as show business itself.

Your Reaction   The first sign of trouble is usually a call or letter from the school. Your reaction is either anger or guilt, neither of which gets you anywhere. Some parents even get nervous when they are called in to talk it over with the teacher or the principal, suffering flashbacks of their own misspent youth ("Please don't tell my parents!"). Sometimes the parents and the teacher blame each other for the problem, creating another damaged relationship. Even worse, kids who act up usually aren't paying that much attention, so their grades go into the dumpster. You want your kids to behave at school, but you can't be there to help them.

Your Strategy   *Establish a good three-way relationship between the teacher, the child, and yourself. As a team, work on recognizing the child's strengths and giving them leadership in areas or projects they are good at.*

What to Try First   The best strategy comes in two stages:

1. Organize a meeting to be attended by you, the child, and the teacher. (NOTE: If the teacher has other ideas, you and your child will have to do the following on your own.)

148

2. Come up with mutually acceptable ways of giving your child significant roles other than, for example, class clown. And agree on consequences if the misbehaviour continues. For example, if she's being disruptive, give her a consequence: maybe she should do her work in the office or another classroom, where she won't disrupt the other students.

The Practical Stuff

✓ Make sure this meeting of the minds is non-confrontational, and conducted with the understanding that you are all working towards a common goal. The first step is to state the problem. Then everyone has a go at finding a solution.

KEY POINT The trick here is to include the child — ask her what she thinks about the problem. What does she think could be done about it? Use reflective listening techniques (see **#5**) to let her know that she's being heard, and that the adults won't gang up on her or punish her. Remember, whether she is right or wrong is really beside the point. The real goal is getting her to agree to a solution.

✓ If she has trouble opening up, let her know that you really want to hear her point of view, and that it's hard to solve the problem without *her* ideas.

✓ The end result of this meeting should be a contract — a written agreement, signed by the child and the teacher, that establishes what they both will and won't do.

ANOTHER KEY POINT Don't aim for perfection, just improvement. Keep it reasonable — if she talks out of turn twenty times a day, start by asking her to reduce that number to ten.

✓ You could also suggest the teacher use a class meeting (if she's into it), so the entire class can work on solving the problem.

✓ Everybody excels at at least one thing. It is up to you and the teacher to find out what your kid is good at, and use it for all it's worth.

• If she's artistic, give her a giant mural to paint or direct.
• If she has leadership qualities, make her a

hall monitor.

- If she is a third-grader that reads well, have her go down to the first grade and read to them.
- If she's a math whiz, let her tutor another child who is a math klutz. Take advantage of the fact that kids are great teachers.

Do's

✓ Do try a private tutor (maybe a local teen-ager) if grades become a real problem. When the grades improve, so should the over-the-top behaviour.

✓ Do ask her to keep a journal of her progress. Go over it with her once in a while.

Don'ts

✗ Don't get mad at her if she has a relapse. It will just make her feel worse about herself. After all, she often doesn't even know why she's doing it.

✗ Don't constantly take her behavioural temperature: "How were you in school today?" It implies that you suspect she hasn't or can't pull it off.

32

HOMEWORK STRUGGLES
2 + 2 = "I'm Not Doing It!"

The Behaviour   Kids are like adults — after they work they want to come home and relax. But children are burdened with this thing called "homework," the reason for which no kid has ever understood. To get out of doing it, kids pull every excuse from their bag of tricks: "I'm tired." "I can't do it." "I'm sick." Or that old standby: "I, um, I *forgot* it. Yeah, that's it."

Why They Do It   They're human, that's why. And human beings are natural procrastinators who would rather play than work. Kids often don't understand why homework is important, or that learning can be fun. After being trapped between the four walls of the classroom all day, the last thing they want is to crack another book. They mean well, but every night they get distracted by TV or each other.

Your Reaction

After a long hard day yourself, you have to become the Homework Police. You also have to assume the role of teacher, struggling to help your kid learn some new kind of math that's baffling even to you. Homework is *their* job, so why do you feel so frustrated when they don't do it?

Your Strategy

The daily routine should be work before play. In any case, make it their responsibility to do their homework.

What to Try First

The trick to getting something done everyday is making it part of a routine. Your child shouldn't even have to think about *when* to do it. Have a meeting with them to schedule a specific time: right after school (often the best solution, since it gets homework out of the way); after dinner; or before or after their favourite TV program. Don't get into a power struggle over it. If they still won't do it, talk to the teacher about possible consequences, which could include everything from homework detention to the wrath of the teacher. The ultimate consequence, however, is lower grades. NOTE: It's important that the consequences happen at school — where the assignment was given — rather than at home.

The Practical Stuff

✓ Cut back on TV, the great seducer of homework-weary kids. Work with them to carve out some TV-free time — perhaps no TV after 5:30. This is much easier to enforce when you include them in coming up with the schedule.

✓ Teach your kids the purpose of homework, which is to reinforce what they learned at school that day. At least they'll understand that it's not just something cooked up by the adults to ruin their evenings.

✓ Teach your child this truism about work — that if you don't do it one day, you have to make it up the next. In adult life, it almost never works to tell your boss you didn't do your work because you were watching cartoons.

✓ If they are having trouble with their homework, say encouraging things like: "This *is* tricky. Let's work on it together" or "You've really been improving. Look how far you've come."

✓ Encourage them to let their teacher know if some aspects of their homework are too hard for them.

KEY POINT You should be there to help them, but don't get tricked into doing it for them. After all, you probably already know how to do it. Instead of telling them how to spell "rhinoceros," show them how to look it up in the dictionary.

The Parent as Teacher Test

Because most parents have never been trained to be teachers, they can become easily frustrated or overly demanding when trying to help with homework. This can harm both the relationship between parent and child, and the child's perception of the learning process. If you don't think you can teach your child without flipping out, get someone else — your spouse, an older sibling, or a tutor — to help instead. To see how suitable you might be, ask yourself these questions:

- Would you feel frustrated if he is not catching on?
- Do you consider yourself a critical person?
- Do you often sigh in exasperation or roll your eyes?
- Are you likely to say things like: "You're not trying. Pay attention!" or "You're not getting up until this is finished!"?

If the answer to any or all of these is yes, maybe you should read the paper in the evenings and let someone else struggle with geometry.

33

LATE FOR SCHOOL
Getting Them out the Door

The Behaviour   Meeting deadlines is hard, but making your *kids* meet a deadline can be excruciating. Getting them off to school is the most challenging deadline of all. With one eye on the time and the other on a growing mound of peanut butter sandwiches, you spend your mornings shouting threats, invectives, and time checks at your family. Your son keeps falling back to sleep and your daughter has changed her clothes for the fifth time. The more you push, the slower they seem to go, until children who normally insist on running everywhere are moving in slow motion. Fuelled by the tyranny of the kitchen clock, you scramble to get ready, but it's no use — you're stressed, they're late for school, and the day is off to a decidedly bad start.

Why They Do It

There are many possible explanations for this behaviour, ranging from a simple power struggle to a fear of going to school. However, you can usually attribute lateness of this kind to the fact that young children have a very fuzzy understanding of time (see also **#1**, on dawdling).

Your Reaction

Not only do you feel responsible for getting them to school on time, but you have your own job to get to. With every tick of the clock, the pressure increases, until everyone is wound up tighter than a drumhead. You're ready for bed, and the day has yet to begin.

Your Strategy

Set up a well-organized morning routine and make sure you leave enough time to carry it out.

What to Try First

Have a family meeting and set up a morning routine that everyone can live with. Make sure to get the kids up at least an hour before you have to

leave so they have time to get ready. The equation goes like this: The less time you have, the more pressure you feel, and the more pressure you feel, the more controlling you get. Your kids in turn respond to your controlling behaviour by rebelling.

The Practical Stuff

✓ One of our saving graces as human beings is our need to feel useful. Have each child choose a task so they are part of the routine. If they are old enough, have one set the table and another prepare breakfast. This way everyone is depending on *them* for something.

✓ Keep morning activity streamlined and simple. Few people are good decision-makers just moments after regaining consciousness, so make sure your kids choose what they will wear the night before. They can also make their lunches and set the breakfast table before they go to bed.

✓ Toddlers have absolutely no sense of time. You have to be with them for each step, but try to use as few reminders as possible. By constantly nagging them to "come on, get dressed" or "hurry, we're late," you may just make your little tyke "parent deaf." Move them to action by standing by the door and putting *your* coat on.

✓ For older kids, tell them you are going and then go sit in the car. Don't worry, they'll come. Few can resist the subtle pressure of someone waiting.

✓ Give them an alarm clock and teach them to tell time. That way they know when they are running late, saving you from yelling yourself hoarse.

✓ Talk to your kids about why they have to be on time. Explain that punctuality is a contribution to the family, and that without it, everyone suffers. Don't preach. Ask questions like: "Is it important that we get out the door on time? Why? What would happen if we are late?" Let them reveal the answers.

Consequences   For best results, make it *their* responsibility to be on time. To achieve this you must make sure they bear the consequences of being late. Here are some ways to do that:

- Talk to their teacher and explain that you are having trouble getting your child out the door. Usually the school will have some kind of consequence — a missed recess or a detention — if they are late.
- For younger children who won't get dressed, take them as they are with their school clothes in a bag. Tell the day care people not to be surprised if your child shows up in pyjamas and must change at school. One taste of this is usually enough.

- Working parents who have their own schedules may need to hire a baby sitter for their slowpoke kid. The baby sitter will take the child to school, where the child will experience the consequences of being late. You should only have to resort to this a few times before the problem is solved.
- If they don't have time for breakfast, or if they forget their lunch, they are hungry.
- If you drive them to school on your way to work, don't accommodate their lateness — make them walk.

34

POOR GRADES
The Report Card from Hell

The Behaviour   It's become a cliché in films and cartoons. The kid comes home with a bad report card — all Ds — head hung low in front of fuming parents. Punishments inevitably follow. It's cute when Norman Rockwell paints it, but in real life it's a drag. Failure and despair hang over the house like a bad smell.

Why They Do It   There may be a very good reason for poor school performance. Perhaps your child has poor vision, or hearing, or even a learning disability. But other, more mundane reasons could also be the cause — poor study habits, a mismatch in teaching methods, discouragement, or pampering parents who have led their child to believe that all things in life will come to those who ask.

Your Reaction

Your kid is blowing her first big test and, as a parent, so are you. Anger and guilt fight for control in a game where everyone loses.

Your Strategy

Separate the "doer from the deed" so your child doesn't feel as bad about himself as he does about his grades. Then, do everything you can to foster a love of learning.

What to Try First

Be encouraging. Bad grades can trap a child in a vicious circle — she feels stupid because she's not doing well, and her feelings of inadequacy make her do even worse. The fact is that kids have a natural tendency to connect their identity to their performance. But a bad grade doesn't mean a child is stupid; she might have missed a crucial lesson, or maybe the teaching method is wrong (some kids are more visual than auditory, or vice versa). A bad grade can actually be helpful because it shows you where the work is needed.

The worst thing you can do is be critical. You have to help her regain her natural love of learning. Don't discourage her by suggesting she's "just not very good at math." Comments like that quickly become self-fulfilling prophecies.

The Practical Stuff

✓ Show an interest in what she is learning, not just in her marks. Do you know why the sky is blue? Probably not. Why not try learning why together?

✓ Make learning look like fun and not so much

like pushing rocks up a hill. Tell your kids what you like to read, what you like to learn, what really amazes you about life.

✓ Tutoring is a great idea. It allows your child to catch up and feel better about himself. And the tutor is not emotionally involved like you are.

✓ Emphasize effort, not results.

✓ Make sure they aren't involved in so many extra-curricular activities that their school work is suffering.

✓ If you have very high expectations and/or little patience, maybe you shouldn't be the one who helps with homework. If you get frustrated and angry, the kid will get discouraged, and you may do damage to your relationship (see #32 on homework struggles).

✓ Find activities that aren't academic but which can teach your kid about important concepts. For example, baking can be used to learn math, conversions, and measuring (and you get muffins out of the deal, too).

✓ Go in and talk to the teacher to see what can be done to improve your child's grades, but make sure you include the child in the discussion. Come up with a plan — maybe he has to work on math every night whether there is homework or not. Get him to agree or it won't work.

✓ Be optimistic. Don't worry (at least not out loud). And let your kid know that you won't give up on him.

✓ Have some empathy. You can quit your job, but a grade-schooler has to go in every day even though he's not doing well.

✓ Don't make a big deal about a sibling who *is* doing well in school (unless you want to start a family feud).

✓ Check with a doctor to make sure there is nothing wrong with your child's hearing or vision.

✓ If you think your child might have a learning disability, ask the school how to have him evaluated.

KEY POINT Emphasize what is going well. If they get five out of ten on a test, point out the five they got right. Tell them it shows they can learn.

35

TEACHER TROUBLE
The Worm in the Apple

The Behaviour   For about six hours a day, five days a week, your child and her teacher are thrown together in the volatile cauldron of the classroom. If they dislike each other, life is not fun.

Why They Do It   Since both are human, they probably both have legitimate beefs. Your child may feel the teacher picks on her, is overly critical, and doesn't get her jokes. The teacher, who has thirty other kids who also want her complete attention, might feel your kid is overly aggressive or, conversely, sucks up obnoxiously. Some people just make a bad match, like the teacher who needs to have control and the kid who craves excitement. It's like a bad marriage.

Your Reaction   Her grades are suffering — she's miserable and so are you. You don't know whether to take sides or change schools. You're trapped between a rock and your own flesh and blood.

Your Strategy   *Be supportive of your child but don't take sides.*

What to Try First   Your job is to help your child solve the problem, not to try and solve it yourself. Your child has to learn to get along with people, especially those in authority, so it won't help if you go to the teacher first to try and sort it out. You want your kid to have the skill and the courage to talk to the teacher herself. And don't take sides — as hard as this is, you have to realize that it's *their* problem.

The Practical Stuff   ✓ Give your complete attention to what your kid says about her problem. Even more importantly, give credence to what she says.

✓ Come up with possible solutions together. Help her see the teacher's side of the problem (how would *she* like to try and control thirty of her peers?). What can she do to be helpful to the teacher?

✓ Teach your child how to be open and articulate about her problems. Role play a meeting with the teacher (you play the part of the teacher). Get her to tell the teacher (in this case, you) what her feelings are: "I feel you don't like me. I feel that whenever something goes wrong, I get nailed for it."

✓ Arrange a meeting between your child and the teacher. You should act as the mediator at this meeting, by being impartial and by trying to get both parties to find a solution. Make sure you don't lay the blame on anyone.

✓ Have the child draw up a contract with the teacher, listing ways she is willing to improve her classroom behaviour.

✓ If attempts to work with just the teacher fail, use the resources of the school by bringing in the principal or a counsellor.

The Divorce

Sometimes a teacher and a student will simply dislike each other so much it can become harmful to the child. As a last resort, it may be best to end the relationship and move your child to another class.

36

WON'T GO TO SCHOOL
Dropping Out of Grade Two

The Behaviour Refusing to go to school can be *the* power struggle of early childhood. In fact, if you're not careful, it can stretch all the way to university. This behaviour is different from merely dawdling (see **#1**), or just being late (**#33**), although there is considerable overlap in both the behaviour and the strategies used — so read both these chapters, as well as Teacher Trouble (**#35**). The point is, when he refuses to go, he is telling you: "I'm not going to school and you can't make me!" While lateness is annoying, not arriving *at all* is simply intolerable.

Why They Do It It could be a power struggle, but most often it's because there is a specific problem at school, such as a fear of being bullied, or a particularly bad relationship with a teacher.

Your Reaction

You quickly learn how hard it is to make a child do something he doesn't want to do. Screams, dire threats, extravagant promises — all fail. Short of throwing them over your shoulder, how can you get a reluctant kid out the door and off to school?

Your Strategy

There is always a reason — find out what it is.

What to Try First

Narrow it down. Here are the top six reasons kids won't go to school:

1. Social problems with other kids.
2. Trouble with the teacher.
3. Academic problems.
4. Anxiety over leaving the nest.
5. Boredom.
6. Power struggle with parents. Refusing to go to school is guaranteed to start a fight.

HELPFUL HINT When you ask why they don't want to go to school, be prepared for a sullen shrug and the mumbled reply: "I don't know." At this point you might have to resort to guessing: "Are you having problems with your friends or your teacher? Are you bored?" If this doesn't get you anywhere, try asking his siblings or friends.

The Practical Stuff

✓ Once you know the problem, you can solve it. If it's an academic problem, make an appointment with the teacher and get to the root of it. You may have to hire a tutor to help, or simply assign extra homework. Have the teacher ask the class who would like to help your child with his history. Ask him who he would like to work with. Give him a choice.

✓ The teacher can also help if it's a social problem. If your child has trouble making friends, the teacher can ask the class if anyone would like to be his friend, or may know of a group that would accept him.

✓ Make sure there are no medical problems, such as poor eyesight or hearing.

✓ Kids do better when their parents take an interest in their school. Join the Home and School Association, volunteer as a teacher of special subjects like computers or music, help supervise field trips, or just come in and tell the class what you do.

Do's

✓ Do make it fun. Create a positive feeling about school in your home. Avoid remarks like: "Yeah, school is a drag, at least it was for me. But you have to do it anyway." Instead, get them excited about school and the idea of learning. If they have a special interest, like reading or nature, help them explore it with field trips, computer software, or special projects (who knows how many Nobel prize winners started by growing roots on a carrot in a glass of water?).

✓ Do have faith in them. Kids who don't like school are frequently discouraged. Let them know you believe they can get along, learn, and succeed.

Don'ts

✗ Don't emphasize grades. If they obsess about getting all As, they can become discouraged even when doing perfectly acceptable work.

37

TROUBLE MAKING FRIENDS
Can't Buy Me Love

The Behaviour The school yard really is like the jungle, where the weak — if not actually eaten — are forced to stand alone over by the fence.

Why They Do It Some kids are too bossy, overly aggressive, or won't play by the rules that make life on the playground bearable. Some simply lack social graces, are painfully shy, or are just too eccentric even for the recess crowd. Then there is the "geek factor" — some kids can get hooked on using strange voices (usually high and screechy). Others wear funny clothes, are only interested in one area (computers or Superman comics), are oblivious to what's hip, or are perhaps a little ripe from lack of personal hygiene. And some schoolyard cliques are impossible to break into.

Your Reaction

Whatever the reason for your child's awkwardness, you feel worried, frustrated, and often overly critical. You may even reject the kid yourself for being obnoxious ("I love him, but sometimes I don't like him"). We are such social animals that it is excruciating to see your child rejected by the group and unable to make friends. Life is hard enough without being the pariah of the second grade.

Your Strategy

One way or another, inappropriate behaviour is a form of overcompensation. These kids need to build up their self-image.

What to Try First

You need to teach your child about socially acceptable behaviour, and you'll need help to do it. Get his siblings together at a family meeting and discuss what it is they all like about each other. Keep it positive. Another approach is to find a kid who is well-liked and enlist his support in bringing your child into the group.

The Practical Stuff

✓ Ask the teacher to stage discussions in the classroom about how to make friends and how to be understanding. Unless your child is braver than most of us and actually *wants* to talk about it in public, make sure the teacher talks in general terms. The questions could include: "Is anyone having a problem? What could we do if someone is being picked on?" Usually the younger the child is, the more open they will be. (See also #23, on shyness, for related advice.)

✓ Concentrate on their strengths. If your child feels unattractive, let them know that character is more important than looks. Point out that they are smart or have many interests. Don't brush off their concerns — they're real — but do teach them the real essence of friendship.

✓ Point out that everyone feels lonely sometimes.

✓ Keep in mind that having one friend is good enough. If your child has made a connection with any other kid, do everything you can to cultivate this budding friendship. Have sleepovers and include the friend in family outings.

✓ If poor hygiene is causing the problem, talk about it in a friendly way (see **#15** for strategies to improve hygiene habits).

KEY POINT If your child is acting weird or is socially uncomfortable, it probably means they lack self-confidence. The cure for this is to figure out why they feel this way. Then, try to build them up. The rule is: *You can't build on weaknesses, only on strengths.* For this reason, you should never criticize. Don't say things like: "You're sloppy" or "You look awful in that outfit — no wonder nobody likes you." Maybe your standards are too high and you criticize too much. Even such seemingly innocent remarks as "You could have done better" will be construed as criticism by your child.

At the
Table

38

TABLE MANNERS
"Stop Dribbling Your Meatballs!"

The Behaviour You would like dinner at your house to be like something out of *Leave it to Beaver*. Instead, it resembles the food-fight scene in *National Lampoon's Animal House*, with kids playing ingenious foodgames, chewing with their mouths open, throwing, grabbing, spilling, and repeatedly getting up and running off. There's a lot going on but not much of it is civilized eating.

Why They Do It The short answer is that most kids can't summon up the patience it takes to sit still for more than five minutes. And the younger they are, the harder it is. They are all together, bursting with energy, and fuelled by a sublime antipathy towards food in general. If there is a general lack of rules in your family, it will show up glaringly at the dinner table.

Your Reaction   Instead of enjoying your meal, you end up trying to control a three-ring circus. How can you teach your kids manners and save your digestion?

Your Strategy   *If they can't act civilized they can't eat at the table. Send them to eat in their room or let them go hungry.*

What to Try First   Obviously, you need some rules. You can decide as a family what the rules are. Just make sure you use them to teach your kids to be considerate of others, which is what "having good manners" is all about. The dinner table is social, after all, and a great place to learn how to talk and listen. Try one of these three alternatives if they misbehave:

1. Ask them to leave the room. Tell them they can come back if they settle down. This gives them a choice.
2. Wordlessly take their plate away (they'll know why). The message here is: "I guess you're not hungry. Let's see how you do next time."
3. Take your own dinner to your room and have a nice quiet meal (this really bugs them).

The Practical Stuff   There are five secrets to a well-mannered meal:

1. First, have a meeting with the kids and discuss why you need rules like "elbows off the table," "no burping," and "no TV during meals." See mistakes as an opportunity to teach manners. For instance, when someone

reaches for the bread and knocks over the gravy boat, it's a good time to make it a rule to ask people to pass things. And don't make small infractions into a big deal. Make sure they take the rules seriously, and be consistent, but don't expect them to be perfect or they will come to hate mealtime.

2. Don't nag — lead. Kids have tremendous powers of observation and they learn by modelling their behaviour after you. Make sure your table manners are up to snuff.

3. Keep mealtimes pleasant. No matter how good the *boeuf bourguignon* is, it won't be enjoyable if you fight or bring up problems. Bring out the fine china and the candles every once in a while — it will appeal to your kids' sense of drama.

4. Include kids in the table talk. They don't like it when parents talk to each other and may act ill-mannered just to bring the focus back to them. This also teaches them how to converse properly. Prime the pump by talking about what happened to you that day, or bring up stuff you know they will be interested in, like plans for the weekend or (everyone's favourite) gossip.

5. Enjoy eating with your kids and let them know it. Be encouraging: "You guys are polite enough to have High Tea with the Queen." Take the older kids to a really fancy restaurant.

39

THE PICKY EATER
Fear of Broccoli

The Behaviour You spend a lot of time planning tasty, nutritious meals for your family. But when you put one of your creations on the table, your kids treat it like green slime. Even your *pasta primavera* grosses them out. Some kids want to skip dinner and only eat fun snacks. Others will literally only eat one or two things — like baloney or peanut butter. And *nobody* under the age of twenty likes brussels sprouts.

Why They Do It Maybe it's a lack of sensuality, or an overabundance of taste buds — whatever the reason, most kids just aren't into food. They also don't have the patience to sit down and do something (like eat a whole meal) for more than a few minutes, preferring to graze on finger food from the fridge all day.

Your Reaction

You know nutrition is vital for growing children, but yours don't seem to be getting enough. It is so emotionally painful when your child won't eat that tensions around the dinner table ruin everyone's digestion.

Your Strategy

Your job is to provide well-balanced meals. It's up to your child to decide whether or not to eat them.

What to Try First

Okay, so you've made dinner and listened to your kids trash it. Here's what you do. Tell them the truth — that you are sorry that they don't like what you made for dinner, and reiterate that it's up to them whether to eat it or not. Don't get caught in an argument. Always try to keep mealtimes pleasant. Don't spoil the mood by trying to force your kids to eat. If they won't eat, assume they are not hungry and ask if they would like you to save the meal for later. Put their uneaten meals in the fridge and forget about it. And don't force them to eat it for breakfast unless you want a protracted power struggle on your hands.

The Practical Stuff

✓ Mealtime problems can be minimized by teaching your kids about food and how important it is (a regular, weekly family meeting is the best time for this). Find out what they like to eat and include them in planning menus and even cooking.

✓ Get them to agree to try certain foods they don't like; experts tell us that kids may have to try a new food up to thirty times before they start to like it. Also, try not to keep too much junk food in the house so your kids won't spoil their appetites.

✓ Kids usually want a snack when they get home from school, but give them too much and the snack becomes dinner. Help them figure out how much is enough to tide them over until mealtime.

Do's

✓ Do serve a variety of foods at each meal. At the very least, it will increase the likelihood that you'll hit on a food your picky eater will like.

✓ Do keep the table conversation abundant and pleasant. This is not a good time to lecture or scold. Remember, this is quality time. Make meals a positive experience for your family and they will look forward to them.

✓ Do have special dinners occasionally. Put a blanket on the living room floor and have a picnic. Or stage a formal dinner in the dining room complete with candles and good china. This will reinforce the idea that meals are fun.

Don'ts

✗ Don't comment on how well or poorly they are eating.

✗ Don't make special meals for the picky eater

(like chicken for everyone else but a side order of Beefaroni for Suzy). This is disrespectful of your time and energy, and gives children the erroneous message that they can always get what they want — as if life were one big restaurant.

✗ Don't get obsessive and start counting mouthfuls. Relax.

Don't Worry

Nutritionists tell us that what your child ate today is less important than what they ate all week. Missing one or two meals, or skipping the broccoli at dinner, is not the end of the world. Look at the big picture before you assume they are not eating properly.

To be totally assured, take your child to a pediatrician to make sure they are growing normally, with no vitamin deficiencies or weight loss.

And remember, it's hard to see your kids go hungry, but hunger is the natural consequence of not eating dinner, and it is a powerful teacher.

40

THE OVERWEIGHT CHILD
Too Much of a Good Thing

The Behaviour

Most parents have a hard time getting their kids to eat, but some face the opposite problem: the child who eats (and eats and eats) to the point of being noticeably overweight.

We're not talking about kids with hormonal problems — that should be dealt with by a doctor. Rather, we mean the kids who just won't stop eating. They load up on junk food, eat between meals, and pig out at parties. It's as if their "full" button doesn't work, so the flow of cheesies, Ding Dongs, and ice cream doesn't stop until the parents force the issue.

The overweight child has one strike against him or her right off the bat. The other kids — who can be as cruel as they are clever — tease mercilessly. Even adults can be prejudiced against a "fat" child.

The overweight child can't keep up with the other kids in sports or on the playground, and may become withdrawn, their self-esteem devastated. The heavier they become, the less interest they have in physical activity. It can become a vicious circle.

Why They Do It

Ask yourself: Why is my kid fat? Is there a lot of pressure in my house to look good? This emphasis on skinniness can backfire. A kid who won't ever be naturally thin may despair of ever reaching this idealized goal and may rebel against it by eating more. Other chubby kids have been pampered. The parents don't want to say no and, unfortunately, a depressingly high percentage of food that tastes good is not good for you. Some kids get used to having what they want when they want it.

Your Reaction

Although parents of picky eaters may joke that this is a problem they would kill for, in reality it's no joke for the child or the parent.

Your Strategy

Don't force them to lose weight. Let them know it's their responsibility to eat properly.

What to Try First

First of all you should talk to a doctor to:

- make sure the extra weight is not a medical problem;
- help come up with a safe, practical eating plan. Remember, dieting — especially with young girls — can be taken to extremes.

Next, get your child involved in the planning of a sensible diet. If they are eight years old or older, teach them about food and nutrition. For instance: what *is* low-fat ice cream and how do you shop for it? Is low-fat frozen yogurt an alternative? See if your local board of health offers supermarket tours to teach people how to shop and eat healthfully. You may even learn something about healthy eating yourself.

Then, get your child to agree to a realistic, long-term weight loss goal. But don't be a food fascist and cut out *all* the good stuff — let them have cake on birthdays and other special occasions. Slacking off occasionally is part of being "realistic."

The Practical Stuff

✓ As any adult who has tried to lose weight knows, motivation is the key to shedding pounds. If the child is not involved from the very start, the whole thing is doomed. They have to understand that this is their body. They have to want to lose the weight. Ironically, the more teasing they get, the worse they feel about themselves, and the less motivated they are to minimize the flab.

✓ After you've convinced your kid to take responsibility, it's time for *you* to take some. Realize that you are a role model for your children. Take a good, hard look at your own diet and what you have in your pantry. Throw out the potato chips and purge your home of Twinkies. Make sure there are lots of fruits and vegetables in the house and tell your pudgy progeny to eat as much of this kind of food as they want. If you have time, cook more of your own foods rather than pre-made convenience foods, which are often high in fat and sugar. Remember, you can make your own home-made muffins and chicken fingers without a zillion fattening additives.

✓ Realize that it's not your job to make your kid happy all of the time; in fact, in the long run always getting what you want can make you *un*happy. Instant gratification only works for that particular instant. But there are a lot of "NOs" in life that pampered people have trouble dealing with. Want to really do your kids a favour? Teach them self-discipline.

✓ Many researchers feel that exercise is at least as important as controlling food intake. You can help your kid by engaging the whole family in some kind of physical activity. Let her see you going for long walks, or doing the odd push-up. Make sure you don't drive everywhere. Unplug the TV and encourage her to walk the dog or go to the market on foot. Swimming can be a great way for heavy kids to exercise. Find fun ways to create an active lifestyle — play frisbee or go on scenic hikes.

Dieting Don'ts

✗ Don't try to control their eating program. They have to take the responsibility or it won't work. If you nag they will rebel and sneak food. Work together to overcome the problem.

✗ Don't go overboard. Your child's natural weight might not be that thin.

✗ Don't comment on their weight too much. When you do, give them words of encouragement like: "Hey, you're really watching what you eat" or "You're really trying hard to eat right." Conversely, comments like "You still look kind of fat. You should try harder" will only make them feel bad and drive them to eat as a consolation.

THOSE
BEDTIME
BLUES

41

BED INVASIONS
Night of the Living Kids

The Behaviour   As a parent, your final refuge from the trials and torments of life is your bed. Surrounded as you are by flannel sheets and sweet dreams, there is nothing worse than being woken up by a child who wants to share it with you.

Why They Do It   Sometimes kids just want to cuddle for a while, but we have also heard of children literally kicking one of the parents (usually the father) right out of bed. A working dad may even throw in the towel and go sleep in the kid's bed. The underlying reason kids want to sleep with you is that they feel safe in your bed. A lot of their fears and anxieties come out at night. If they don't feel they can handle it on their own, they quite naturally come looking for you.

Your Reaction

For most hard-working parents, bed invasions are a major inconvenience. Even if you like occasionally sleeping with your children, they are more active than adults, even at night. They wriggle and talk and sneeze and sleep sideways, and it usually just doesn't work. Whether it's because of a loud thunderstorm or loneliness, a nocturnal bed invasion means that nobody is getting enough sleep. Discouraging it without a major battle is a tricky problem in the middle of the night.

Your Strategy

Let it be known that you will defend your right to the only thirty-six square feet in the house that are truly yours.

What to Try First

You and your partner have to be truly committed to the idea that the kids don't sleep in your bed. Tell your kids in no uncertain terms that, except in emergencies, you sleep in your bed and they sleep in theirs. Period. Look upon this as a terrific chance to teach your kids respect for the rights of others.

The Practical Stuff

As with all parenting situations, you have to be firm and consistent. In a committed tone of voice, tell them that if they come to you in the night, you will put them back. It's hard to be firm when you're three-quarters asleep, but give in once and you can expect that dreaded tap on the shoulder for many nights to come.

Expect to be driven to great lengths in the protection of your space. Some parents don't know the child has slipped into their bed until the morning, when they roll over onto that little lump in the middle. Pile up something that will make a noise in front of your door if it is opened, like tin cans, or tie a bell to the handle. Forewarned is forearmed.

If you feel it's wrong to deny your children the comfort of your bed, remember that what you are really doing is teaching them how to go to sleep — how to solve their own problems and comfort themselves. After all, as grownups we wake up at times during the night; we've had to learn how to put ourselves back into dreamland. If your kids are allowed to come running to you every time they wake up, it will postpone the learning of this essential life skill.

KEY POINT It's not that you don't want them to sleep with you — in other words, it's not a rejection of *them*. Explain to them that rather, you are asserting your right to undisturbed sleep, your own bed, and a modicum of privacy.

Exceptions

Thunderstorms and sicknesses are understandable temptations to break the rules. However, no matter how comforting it is for that night, you might have to spend a week getting them back on track. You can, however, stay with them in their room until the storm blows over or the fever breaks. Just make sure they know you are always there to defend them against infections, atmospheric commotions, and the monster who lives in their closet.

Of course, you don't want your off-limits policy to get in the way of morning cuddles. As long as they don't disturb your sleep or your space, this is too good a time for affection to give up.

Another possible exception is the "family bed," a recent phenomenon where the entire family sleeps together. Our view is, if you really want to sleep the way they did in the 12th century, why not?

42

BED-WETTING
The Chill of the Night

The Behaviour
Most parents just *love* getting up in the middle of the night, with their head full of dreams and their eyes glued shut, to change a bed full of wet pee. Kids as old as ten or eleven can have these nocturnal accidents, which can be particularly embarrassing for them when they sleep over at a friend's house.

Why They Do It
The most important thing to realize is that in almost every case, they are not wetting the bed deliberately. It's not their fault. Think about it: who would turn their warm, cozy bed into a clammy swamp on purpose?

Some theorists believe that kids who wet their beds just sleep more soundly than others and don't hear that call of nature. Others blame genetics or a sleep disorder. It could also be a medical problem, so you should talk to your family doctor about it.

Your Reaction

Parents react with either disappointment or anger. They think their child *could* wake up to take care of business in the proper place, but can't be bothered. Some parents even start to flirt with the idea of returning to diapers. How can you help your kids make it through the night?

Your Strategy

Don't get angry. Let them know it's not a big deal and that they will grow out of it.

What to Try First

Realize that they are not doing it on purpose. Since there is really nothing they can do about it, wake them up and put them on the toilet before you go

to bed. BONUS: They look so cute when they're half asleep.

The Practical Stuff

✓ Limit the amount of liquid they drink before they go to bed, starting right after dinner.

✓ Get them to help change the bed and put the sheets in the washer, beginning at about age four. This won't stop them from peeing, but it does help give them some control over the situation.

Limiting the Damage

You're cranky because your sleep has been disturbed, but don't forget that bed-wetting can have a serious, negative effect on your child's self-esteem. Be nice about it — they think there's something wrong with them, and they feel bad enough without being scolded. It's particularly upsetting when their younger siblings have stopped doing it. To maintain their self-esteem:

- Always be encouraging: "I know you tried not to wet the bed."
- Don't be so serious about it. Keep things light.
- Let them know that with time, this too shall pass.

KEY POINT The good news is that nearly all cases disappear by adolescence.

43

WON'T GO TO SLEEP
No Bedtime for Bonzo

The Behaviour   It's the end of the day. You're exhausted and so are
the kids, yet they still have enough manic energy
left to run around after you have put them to bed.
It always happens when you are at your most vulnerable. Just as you sink thankfully into the couch
thinking your day's work is done, a child appears
at the foot of the stairs, grinning impishly. Others
repeatedly call for water, or reassurance, or just
absolutely refuse to get into that bed.

Why They Do It   Calling for water or enticing you to chase them
around the house and put them back to bed is a
great way for a child to get your attention. On the
other hand, a child who refuses to go to bed, or
who keeps getting up, may also be interested in
power.

Your Reaction

You have tried everything from sweet, calm reasoning to bellowed threats, but nothing works. The evening is becoming anything but restful.

Your Strategy

The fact is, kids like routine. It makes them feel safe and secure. So set up a routine and stick to it.

What to Try First

Agree on a bedtime routine (for kids under the age of five, you will have to set the schedule). Decide together what time you will start the bath, read them a story, and turn out the lights. Let's say bedtime is 8 p.m. Start the bath at 7:15 and tell them it's ready. You don't have to be a drill sergeant about it, just be consistent. The logical consequence, if they fool around and won't get in, is that they miss their bath. Don't repeat the invitation, or scold or threaten. Just resolutely move on to the next stage of the routine. Maybe you have scheduled fifteen minutes for story time. If they dawdle, that night's chapter of *Charlotte's Web* is cancelled. The same goes for that most sacred of childhood repasts — the bedtime snack. At eight o'clock sharp the kids are put in their beds and the lights turned off, no matter where they are in the routine. It may take a while to get used to, so expect a few nights of outraged disbelief. You might even have to let them sleep in their clothes. The trick is to avoid getting snared by their ingenious delaying tactics. As soon as they realize you won't spend two hours putting them to bed, they will be more likely to follow the routine. After that, the night will once again belong to you.

The Practical Stuff

The key is to be friendly but firm. Let the kids know exactly what they can expect from you. If they like to call for a glass of water after you have put them down, leave one in their room. Make it clear that after eight o'clock you turn into a couch potato and, quite obviously, will be unable to help them (unless the house catches fire). A younger child may even cry herself to sleep for one or two nights, but be firm and stick to your guns.

The Power Child

Never argue with a child who's into power — it's exactly what they want. Instead, use one of the two following methods:

1. If they come downstairs, act as if they just turned into The Invisible Kid. Watch TV, read a book, and talk to your spouse, but ignore the child. This takes all the fun out of it for them. There is no payoff because they came looking for a fight and you threw in the towel. If they try to climb on you or throw things in order to engage your attention, take a good book into the bathroom and lock the door. Eventually they will get bored and go to bed (you know they're tired, even if they don't).

2. Give them a choice: either they can stay in their room with the door open and the hall light on or, if they keep coming out, you will close the door. Most will prefer the open door. They can read or sing or attend Barbie's wedding if they want to, as long as they stay put.

OUT IN
PUBLIC

44

THE GIMMES
"I Want a Godzilla Pez Dispenser and I Want It Now!"

The Behaviour

It gets so you can't buy a quart of milk without your kid demanding half the candy rack, or come home from a short absence without a toy.

Why They Do It

North Americans live in a big candy store. We are surrounded by all kinds of wonderful products, and we are encouraged by advertising experts to want them, to *need* them. Kids are particularly susceptible to our materialistic culture. They reel away from the TV set, their heads filled with the latest toy and the command: "TELL MOM TO PICK SOME UP TODAY!" They can — for extremely short periods of time — lust after a pencil with a pumpkin-shaped eraser the way you lust after a Mercedes-Benz. They also have no conception of cost. They see it and they want it. If you give it to them they think: "Hey, life is great. All I have to do is whine and make a demanding fuss and I get what I want. Even if I don't get it right away, eventually they cave in and buy it."

Your Reaction

These days, a lot of parents give their kids what they ask for. That's because many of us — particularly working parents who feel guilty about not spending enough time with the kids — are too concerned with making our kids happy. We want to buy them the world and can't stand to see them want for anything. Ironically, by indulging them we may be making our kids unhappy — it's hard to be satisfied when things come too easily. Their enjoyment is in the getting (which is transient) and they turn into an emotional buzz saw that only looks forward to the next "fix."

We all like material things, but how can we raise our kids to have self-restraint in our increasingly material world?

Your Strategy

Remember that kids who get less appreciate more.

What to Try First

Create an environment in your home where ideas and character are more important than possessions, where things are made as often as they are bought, and where gift giving is just as important as gift getting.

The Practical Stuff

✓ Teach them the value of money and how to budget it. Give them an allowance (see **#25** on money matters). Let them save for things they want instead of serving it up on a silver platter. Let them experience *not* having something. FACT: The average North American girl has eight Barbie dolls.

✓ Occasionally watch TV shows and commercials with them (not all the time or you will spoil their fun) and talk about how commercials manipulate people into buying things. Teach them the discrimination and awareness they will need to avoid being passively led by the nose into the *Land of the Next Big Thing.*

✓ Get your kids to make gifts and cards for people instead of buying them. Encourage them to give *you* something for a change. Giving makes us feel good, but kids are seldom asked to do it.

✓ Give to charity. As a family, sponsor a refugee or a poor child overseas. Have the kids collect for UNICEF during Hallowe'en, help donate to food banks, or give some of their surplus toys to needier kids.

✓ Give your kids something to model after. Look at your own materialism. If you constantly buy yourself presents to perk yourself up, why shouldn't your kids do the same thing? Instead, cut off a pair of old pants to make shorts. Let them see you recycling or doing without.

✓ Don't make a big fuss about new items: "Oh! You look *soooo* nice in your new spandex jumpsuit from The Gap." This gives them an insatiable craving for something new, as if clothes could go stale. Draw the line at $300 designer sneakers. In fact, it's probably not a great idea for *you* to make a big deal about designer labels. Some kids will only wear one kind, a sure sign that they have ascended into the upper echelon of materialism.

KEY POINT — MAKE YOUR OWN FUN As anyone who lived through the Great Depression knows, the less you have, the more creative you have to be. Buy your kids Barbie dolls if you must, but suggest that they make their own Barbie clothes, accessories, and homes. Give your kids a box full of paper towel tubes, cloth, tissue paper, paint, and glue so they can make their own puppets. Get your hands on a large cardboard packing crate (from a refrigerator, for example) to use as a puppet theatre. In fact, a great big cardboard box is the greatest toy ever invented. Someone should open a store called Boxes "R" Us.

45

PUBLIC TANTRUMS
Show Time at the Mall

The Behaviour   What parent hasn't endured the humiliation of the supermarket (or parking lot, or sidewalk) tantrum? Red-faced and screaming at the top of their lungs, the little darlings refuse to move, run off out of sight, or throw themselves down onto the pavement. If they're really good at it they can draw a crowd. And how many restaurant meals have been ruined — not just for you but for the entire restaurant — by a two-year-old acting up?

Why They Do It   The fact is, if your child really wants to win a power struggle, the best place to try is out in public. You are at your most vulnerable and they seem to sense that. There are few socially acceptable options open to you. Screaming back merely lowers you to their level. Hitting or dragging them out by the arm is abusive, and appealing to sweet reason is laughably ineffective. No, let's face it — if they decide to play the public tantrum card and you don't know how to handle it, you've had it.

Your Reaction

There are only three ways to stop a tantrum in public: verbal and physical abuse; giving them what they want; or taking them home. Most parents use one of the first two, which won't work in the long term.

Your Strategy

Prevention is the key. Overstimulating them or taking them out when they're tired is asking for trouble.

What to Try First

There's not a lot you *can* try when a three- or four-year-old freaks out in the middle of Wal-Mart and starts screaming for a gingerbread man. Don't bother with idle threats — they don't work. This kid wants that gingerbread man and is prepared to go to the mat to get it. Give them a choice — either calm down or leave. If they don't stop, pick them up without anger (that's the hard part), or lead them by the hand and take them home. Let them know that they can't go out with you until they can behave in public. Get a baby sitter or drop them off with friends next time if you have to. Most importantly, get them to tell *you* when they're ready to try it again. Have faith that they will know when they're ready.

The Practical Stuff

✓ Probably the worst site for a public tantrum is in a restaurant. The younger they are, the

harder it is for kids to sit at a table for two hours and be cooperative. Come prepared with lots of diversions like colouring books. Always include the kids in the conversation. Pick noisy eateries — the kind of place where you have to shout to be heard. Make sure everyone knows the rules beforehand. If they still act up, get them out of there for everyone's sake. You have to be prepared to finish your meal out of a doggy bag at home, but the kids will learn from it. Remember, they don't really want to leave early either. If you mean business and the kids know it, you can be dining in restaurants with white linen and fine china by the time they are six.

✓ Avoid overstimulating them. Even though kids love excitement, it's surprising how quickly they are tired by overstimulation. To avoid voltage overload, don't plan too many events per outing. An hour at the mall is usually enough for very young kids. Definitely don't drag them to two malls, McDonald's, and a movie.

✓ Prepare them to be in public by establishing rules: no running, no whining for things, etc. Ask them if they think they can handle that.

✓ Avoid impulse buying with kids. Decide (with the kids) on what you want to buy *before* you go into the store. This decreases the possibility that they will demand something and freak out when they don't get it.

✓ Engage them in a helpful role. At the supermarket, get them to help put the potatoes in the bag, or play "find the fusilli." At the department store, ask them if they think Grandma would like this colour of tights. This works especially well for attention seekers, because by doing this they have your (positive) attention.

KEY POINT Don't give in just to keep them quiet, or you will reinforce their misbehaviour. This is the hardest part, but kids can sense that you act differently in public, and they're smart enough to take advantage of that.

46

CAR TRAVEL
"Are We There Yet?"

The Behaviour   Ah yes, there's nothing like enclosing the entire family in a tiny little room on wheels for seven or eight hours. Kids, who haven't yet developed their parents' ability to sit quietly and worry about things, feel bored and trapped during long car rides. It also appears that their bladders mysteriously shrink, so they whine and fidget and ask to go to the bathroom every five minutes. The fighting, bickering, and rambunctious play that would normally take place outside or in another room of the house are performed on the back of your neck as you steer the car at sixty miles an hour. Insults and juice cartons whiz past your head.

Why They Do It   Because kids live for the moment, they don't have a very good grasp of abstract concepts like "later."

One result of this is that they sometimes lack patience. They can't conceive of arriving at their destination, so they feel caged, with nothing but their boundless and restless energy to occupy them.

Your Reaction

Tempers flare when you try to discipline the kids and drive at the same time. Worse, only half your concentration is on the road. When kids act up in the car, it's not only annoying, it's dangerous.

Your Strategy

Stop the car and refuse to drive until everyone calms down and acts at least remotely civilized.

What to Try First

Stop telling them what to do and start telling them what *you* will do. The beauty of this approach is that you are being firm while putting the onus on them. It is the classic "I" message. One of these is worth ten admonishments to "shut up, for crying out loud" or "settle down back there."

You can tell them in advance — "I don't want to have an accident so I will stop until it's safe to drive again" — or simply pull over to the side of the road (the best response when kids take off their seat belts). Kids are smart; they'll know why you are stopping. BIG TIP: Plan it. It really helps if you are going someplace the kids are excited about, like the zoo or a friend's place. CAUTION: Don't just crank the wheel over and stop. Watch where you pull off. Take the nearest highway exit, or drive into a parking lot.

The Practical Stuff

✓ Usually, the opening round of the road trip to hell involves fighting over the front seat or access to the window. Prevent this by deciding beforehand — at a family meeting — who sits where. Maybe the kids can come up with rotating seat arrangements. Don't take them anywhere until a deal has been struck. Leave yourself enough time so the kids can negotiate seating arrangements without being rushed. And remember, it's their responsibility to do this, not yours.

✓ Being a mom or dad means carpooling the kids around. You can use the same technique (refusing to drive until things settle down) with other people's kids, but remember to tell the parents what you are doing and that you might be a little late.

HELPFUL HINTS To keep the kids from going snaky during long trips, planning is crucial:

• Recognize your kids' low boredom threshold by making frequent stops and taking interesting routes. Expect an eight-hour ride to take ten with kids.

- Bring games, like portable video games, toys, and dolls.
- Bring books and audio tapes, especially "talking books."
- Bring sandwiches, snacks, and water to drink (spilled water is no problem, but juice and milk can really gum up the upholstery).
- Play standard travel games that have been getting kids from point A to B for decades, like sing-alongs, "I Spy," or "Spot the Car with Roof Racks (or Foreign Plates, or whatever)."

BEYOND THE NUCLEAR FAMILY

47

GRANDPARENTS
The Spoilers

The Behaviour   How many times have you heard this: "It's the grandparents' duty to spoil their grandchildren."

They're not kidding, either. There's no doubt that your parents love your kids. The trouble comes when they try to do more than just dote. Some grandparents criticize how you are raising the kids: "That's not how we raised you and you turned out all right." Or how you dress them — usually not enough socks. You bite your tongue till it bleeds as they reinforce gender stereotypes ("Johnny's going to grow up to be a doctor and Suzy's going to be a nurse.") They stuff your kids full of sugar and buy them anything they want. You spend years teaching your kids about what is right and wrong, carefully choosing consequences, and trying to be consistent, only to have your parents wreck the entire program in a single weekend of late nights and candy floss. Not that any of this is surprising — get any three generations together, and there is enough conflict to keep a team of psychoanalysts busy.

Why They Do It They're having fun, that's why. They get to indulge their favourite children without having to consider the consequences. And after putting up with your guff for a few decades, they probably feel they are experts in the field, and *should* be able to tell you how to raise kids.

Your Reaction You genuinely want your kids to have a good relationship with your parents, but the tension is becoming unbearable.

Your Strategy *Ultimately, you can't control the relationship your parents have with your kids. In essence — mind your own business.*

What to Try First Back off a little. Your kids want, and deserve, a relationship with their grandparents. You have to realize that's just what it is — *their* relationship. Have faith that they can deal with anything (outside of actual abuse) without your constant protection. In fact, your kids can probably take more, overlook more, and forgive more than you can.

HELPFUL HINT If it's too stressful, see them less. Spend time with other people so the effect on your kids is minimized.

The Practical Stuff

✓ Take a good look at your motives. Realize that you might be overcritical of your parents. Maybe you're still playing the old power game, and you're dragging the kids into it. Sometimes you can learn from a different approach. Besides that, involved grandparents almost always enrich a child's life.

✓ Face the fact that you are not necessarily going to change your parents' attitudes towards parenting any more than they are going to change yours. Having said that, if they are open at all, you should try to talk to them about the problems.

IMPORTANT LIFE-SAVING TIP While you are explaining your theories on child-rearing, try to avoid implying that you want to do it differently from them because *they* really screwed up when they raised *you*. If they are *extremely* open, take them to a parenting class and give them a book or two to read.

48

THE NEIGHBOURS
*When the Back Fence Becomes
the Berlin Wall*

The Behaviour   Does the word "feud" mean anything to you?
Except for very loud heavy metal music, nothing
can cause trouble between neighbours faster than
kids. Your kids can bug the guy next door by asking too many questions or committing crimes
against his azaleas. And some neighbours seem to
think it's okay to discipline your kids, while you
wish you could discipline *theirs*.

Why They Do It   The relationship between neighbours and kids is a
subtle one. People who live next door are almost
never strangers, and in fact can be quite close. But
they are never family. The constant low-level interaction can cause friction if the ground rules are not
clearly laid out.

Your Reaction

You are torn between your desire to protect your kids and the red-faced embarrassment you feel when they are bothering someone. Or the shoe may be on the other foot, in which case you wonder if their kids could be sent to obedience school. Dealing with other people's kids over the garden wall can be tricky. If you don't want to move, what's a good neighbour to do?

Your Strategy

Teach your children to be thoughtful neighbours. When the kids next door come to your house, let them know they have to follow your rules.

What to Try First

Next to their immediate family, neighbours are usually the most important people in your kids' outdoor lives. It's important to get along with them. That means everyone has to learn to compromise. Also, while it's good to know what's going on, unless you suspect outright abuse you should try to stay out of it. Let your kids work out any problems themselves. Some parents are too involved in their kids' lives. Besides, these kinds of problems provide a great opportunity to learn how to get along with people — that is, if you're willing to let it happen. If they get temporarily barred from the neighbour's turf, let them experience the consequences. Your kids have to learn to honour the rules of other homes. Without siding with them every time there is a tiff, you should also teach them to stand up for themselves. If it gets chronic, however, it's time to set up a meeting of the minds.

The Practical Stuff

Talk to your kids (while letting them know you are really listening) to identify the problem and some possible solutions. Then, invite the neighbours over with their kids. The timing is important here. Don't try to talk while your neighbours are still sputtering with anger. Let them cool off first, but don't wait too long or resentment will take root. Here's how to have a successful meeting:

✓ Keep it informal — it could literally be over the back fence or on the lawn.

✓ Make it non-confrontational. Don't blame, no matter how justified you might be ("your kid *did*, after all, hit mine with a brick"). Just initiate a civil discussion: "We've noticed there's been a problem. Do you want to talk about it?" Don't get drawn into any arguments — after all, someone has to be the adult here.

✓ Once you agree on the problem, move on to possible solutions. While you're brainstorming, make sure the kids participate. And remember, there really is another side to every story.

✓ If both families have kids, try to agree on ground rules that will cover their interaction.

HELPFUL HINT Teach the neighbours' kids the rules of your house and give them consequences for breaking them. For example: "If you don't stay out of the flower beds, you'll have to go home."

49

THE SINGLE PARENT
When Guilt Is Not Enough

The Behaviour Lots of couples wonder what they would do if one of them wasn't there to help raise the kids. Single parents *know*. Time becomes a commodity more precious than gold — time to get remotely enough sleep, or to go out, or even to take a bath for a few glorious solitary moments.

And then there is the guilt. If they have a job, single moms often try to be both Betty Crocker and Business Woman of the Year. They worry about spending enough time with their kids. They wonder if they are giving their kids enough supervision, and cringe when they think that other people seem to be raising them. If you are divorced, you might feel doubly guilty for causing your child to be without a second parent. After a hard day of singlehandedly doing a job that *two* people find exhausting, you are almost as sorry for your child as you are for yourself. You need help.

Your Strategy

Resist the impulse to pamper your child out of guilt.

What to Try First

Don't feel so sorry for the kid that you overcompensate by always buying them treats, overprotecting them, and letting them run amok. This creates feelings of self-pity and expectation in your child: "Poor me! I'm special. I should be able to do what I want and get what I want."

The Practical Stuff

Face it. You and your kids are in it together. It will be good for you — and very good for them — to let your kids know this so they can take up some of the slack. Sure, this sounds easy, but it's hard to do in real life. See below for some tips on how to make life as the only parent a positive experience rather than a crushing chore.

Do's

✓ Do set up and maintain routines. Routines are efficient and they give kids the parameters they need. Don't let them (or yourself) deviate from the agreed-upon routines because you feel guilty.

✓ Do let your kids know — without being a martyr about it — that you work hard and need their help. One of the most overlooked of children's attributes is that they absolutely *love* to be helpful.

✓ Do have regularly scheduled family meetings. Use this time to work out problems and routines together, as a team.

✓ Do watch out for the signs that you are reaching the breaking point. To avoid them, carve out some time for yourself, no matter how hard it is. The stress of having to do everything can cause you to overreact and make poor decisions. So take the phone off the hook and tell your kids that unless they smell smoke or Robert Redford comes to the door, you are taking a long hot bath and are not to be disturbed for one full rapturous hour. Get them used to Mom disappearing for an hour every few nights. If this doesn't work, see the next item.

✓ Do create an extended family of relatives, friends, baby sitters, older siblings, day care people, other moms — any reliable person with a pulse. Life is a two-way street, so make sure you help your friends as well. Set up a swap system with other moms. You might even want to move in with another single parent family.

✓ Do join or organize a Single Parents' Support Group in your neighbourhood.

✓ Do get help from a counsellor or a family agency if you start to think of your kids as a tremendous burden.

✓ Do take a parenting course. Being a parent is the most important job any of us will ever have. Learn the skills you need to do it well.

✓ Do make a list of priorities. Everyone needs this, but single parents need it more than anyone. Don't try to be perfect and do it all. Maybe you don't have to make the beds in the morning. Think about it — no one dies because a house that is empty all day has unmade beds. Concentrate on what is really important.

Don'ts

✗ Don't try to make up for lost time with goodies and special privileges.

✗ Don't let them break the family routine. "I want to stay up late to see you" is hard to resist, but resist it you must. He is playing on your guilt like a violin. Besides, he needs his sleep.

✗ Don't feel sorry for your kids because they only have one parent. Pity is discouraging and will make them feel sorry for themselves.

Benefits of Single Parenting (No Kidding)

Believe it or not, single-parent families can actually work better than the two-parent variety. Here's how:

- Single parents can have a very close relationship with their kids.
- A lot of single moms and dads (and there are more and more single dads out there) are so

busy they literally don't have time to lavish attention on their child. This makes pampering impossible and results in a more independent child.

- A lot of spouses argue over how to raise the child. If you're single, what you say goes. It's easier to be consistent without someone else throwing you off your game plan.
- If you haven't pampered them, your kids will pitch in and help, recognizing that some days you are like a hamster on a treadmill.
- You'll have a greater sense of accomplishment when you inevitably pull it off.

50

STEPPARENTS AND STEPFAMILIES
The Curse of Cinderella

The Behaviour Forming a stepfamily is a process fraught with danger — it's amazing, considering how much could go wrong, that so many manage to make it work and even thrive. Whether the vacancy you are filling came about by death or divorce, if you're not careful your entry into the family can be like walking into a spinning propeller. For one thing, your stepchild might not recognize your authority. Or he might have enjoyed having his mom or dad all to himself until *you* showed up. On the other hand, maybe you don't like him — or his habits. He might go to bed at 11:30 but you feel that a seven-year-old should be in bed by eight. If you are bringing your own family with you into the relationship, your new spouse's kids might not like them, and the feeling might be mutual.

Why They Do It

The family is the rock that shelters us from an ever-changing, sometimes frightening world. It's very disruptive when something radical happens to the family makeup. As the incoming parent, you may have the best intentions in the world, but the potential is always there for your arrival to look like an invasion.

Your Reaction

You try to make it all work, but rejection is hard to take. The mix-and-match family is so charged with conflicting emotions and subplots, it can be like living inside a cheap novel. The question is, how do you give it a happy ending?

Your Strategy

Concentrate on conflict resolution and communication skills. Never have family meetings been so important to family happiness.

What to Try First

Have lots of family meetings, but don't expect it to be easy. Integrating yourself into a new family will take generous amounts of the three Ps: patience, planning, and problem solving. And the meetings — involving everyone concerned — should begin well before you move in. You can't have enough of these meetings. They are used to hammer out the details of the new routines and decide which of the old ones can be kept (TIP: Try to keep the routines the kids like). Don't come in and reinvent their universe. When you do have to make changes, do it as tactfully as possible. After the intense first stage is over, hold these family meetings once a week for the life of the family.

The Practical Stuff

✓ Give your stepkids as much control as you can. They're probably feeling rather overwhelmed and helpless — after all, how would you feel if your child suddenly decided to leave for another family, or brought another child in, whether you liked it or not? Try to understand their problems and concerns. Take them seriously — and let them know you understand (see the tips on listening in #5), so they feel they have a chance to make changes or right what they see as wrongs.

✓ If you are replacing a parent who has died, don't try to take their place. Your job is to forge a new relationship based on mutual love and respect.

✓ Learn about your stepkids' interests and dislikes — school, hobbies, movies, etc. Try to have fun with them. But let the kids set the pace. If they are angry or standoffish, let it be. Stay friendly. If you don't force it, they will eventually learn that it's not as bad as they thought.

LOVE IS NOT ENOUGH

If it were enough to simply love our kids, virtually every family would be trouble free. Unfortunately it isn't enough, which is why you have read this book. Love has to come first, but on this foundation must be placed the skills of conflict resolution, consistency, mutual respect, patience, and the ability to be a good listener. It's a lot of hard work to be a good parent, but it's worth it. In fact, we believe that teaching parents the skills they need should be a national priority, with information taught the same way prenatal information is taught — as a matter of course. Until then, read more books about it. Talk to your friends about their problems and solutions. And above all, take a parenting course. If there isn't one in your neighbourhood, ask your local school board or department of health to start one. It could be the best gift you ever give to yourself, and to the ones you love the most.